THE BOOSEY & HAWKES MASTERV

LEONARD BERNSTEIN

ORCHESTRAL ANTHOLOGY • *Volume 2*

ANTHOLOGIE D'ŒUVRES POUR ORCHESTRE • VOLUME 2
ANTHOLOGY VON ORCHESTERWERKEN • BAND 2

Overture to *Candide*
Symphonic Suite from *On the Waterfront*
Prelude, Fugue and Riffs
Divertimento for Orchestra

Boosey & Hawkes Music Publishers Ltd
www.boosey.com

Publisher's note

The publishers have used their best efforts to clear the copyright for images used in this volume with the relevant owners and print suitable acknowledgements. If any copyright owner has not been consulted or an acknowledgement has been omitted, the publishers offer their apologies and will rectify the situation following formal notification.

Cover design by Lynette Williamson
Front cover picture: Max Weber - *New York, 1913*
Thyssen-Bornemisza Collection
Leonard Bernstein® is a registered trademark of Amberson, Inc.
The Leonard Bernstein Music Publishing Company LLC is a venture of Amberson Inc. and PolyGram Music Publishing
Preface © Copyright 1998 by Malcolm MacDonald
Printed and bound in England by Halstan & Co. Ltd, Amersham, Bucks.

Contents

Leonard Bernstein, 1980

(Photo: Clive Barda-PAL)

Preface

Bernstein's *Candide*, an operetta based on Voltaire's satirical novel with libretto by Lillian Hellmann, was composed in 1956 and opened at the Martin Beck Theater, New York, on 1 December. The composer later scored the overture for full orchestra, performing it with the New York Philharmonic on 26 January 1957; since then it has been one of his most frequently heard works. Though breezy and uncomplicated, it contains plenty of musical jokes for the initiated, and contrasts the initial fanfare with a lightning tour of some of the operetta's best-loved numbers. The duet 'Oh Happy we' (bar 83) provides the lyrical second subject, and the sparkling coda, referring to the aria 'Glitter and be Gay', leads into a final section that weaves all the music into a cheerful sign-off.

Considering Bernstein's popularity and media celebrity, it is surprising that he wrote the music to just one motion picture - Elia Kazan's *On the Waterfront* (1954). Featuring the young Marlon Brando, this New York dockland drama is a classic, not least because of the power of Bernstein's score. In 1955 Bernstein extracted a symphonic suite, and conducted the Boston Symphony Orchestra in the premiere at Tanglewood on 11 August. The Suite skilfully incorporates all the themes and textures from the original score into a compelling musical whole which is entirely independent of the film's visual impetus.

Prelude, Fugue and Riffs for clarinet and jazz ensemble received its premiere live on television on 16 October 1955, played by Benny Goodman and his band. (In fact the work was composed in 1949 to a commission from Woody Herman, but it had languished unplayed because Herman had disbanded his group.) The title proclaims the marriage of concert music and jazz, the Baroque form of Prelude and Fugue being complemented by a series of riffs (in jazz parlance, a riff is a short, repeated melodic figure). The Prelude, played by the brass, and the Fugue, for the saxophones, show the imprint of Stravinsky (who had written his own *Ebony Concerto* for Woody Herman in 1946). The solo clarinet does not enter until the Riffs, which it plays in purest jazz style with the backing of the piano and then the entire band, who also bring back the themes of the Prelude and Fugue.

In the *Divertimento*, Bernstein consciously looked back to the irreverent manner of *Candide*. Composed in 1980 for the centenary of the Boston Symphony Orchestra, it is founded on a two-note motif, B-C ("B" for Boston, "C" for Centenary - or 100 in Roman numerals). The opening movement, 'Sennets and Tuckets' (Shakespearean for 'fanfares') was originally intended to be the whole piece, but Bernstein saw so much potential in the material that he wrote eight short movements displaying each section of the orchestra. 'Sennets and Tuckets' exposes the B-C motif immediately on the brass and contains a brief quotation from Stravinsky's *Dumbarton Oaks* - just one of the work's many musical jokes. The Waltz (for strings), in 7/8 time, is a tender parody of Viennese salon style; the Mazurka (double reeds and harp) an evocation of East European music; and the Samba imparts an unexpected Latin flavour. The 'Turkey Trot' is reminiscent of Aaron Copland in rustic mood. 'Sphinxes' contains two statements of a rising 12-note melody, each concluded with a trite diatonic cadence - Mahler and Shostakovich seem likely targets here. The Blues for brass and percussion is one of Bernstein's most sophisticated jazz evocations with, perhaps, a nod to Gershwin's *Porgy and Bess*. The finale, an 'In Memoriam' for former members of the orchestra, begins with a canon for flutes, then launches into an uproarious march, 'The BSO Forever', recalling Sousa's *Stars and Stripes Forever* and also making reference to Johann Strauss's *Radetsky March*.

Malcolm MacDonald

Préface

Candide de Bernstein, une opérette basée sur le roman satirique deVoltaire, dont le livret est de Lilian Hellman, fut composé en 1956 et fut donné pour la première fois au théâtre Martin Beck à NewYork, le 1er décembre de la même année. Le compositeur écrivit plus tard l'ouverture pour orchestre. Le NewYork Philharmonic la joua sous sa direction, le 26 janvier 1957, elle est devenue depuis une de ses œuvres les plus jouées. Bien que enjouée et sans complication, elle recèle, pour l'initié, un grand nombre de plaisanteries musicales et fait contraste entre la fanfare initiale et un tour éclair de certaines des chansons les plus aimées de l'opérette. Le duo "Oh Happy we" (mesure 83) fournit le deuxième sujet, lyrique, la coda éclatante se référant à l'aria "Glitter and be Gay", mène à une section finale qui remanie l'ensemble de l'oeuvre en une conclusion pleine d'entrain.

Lorsque l'on pense à la popularité de Bernstein et à sa célébrité dans les médias, il est surprenant qu'il n'ait écrit qu'une seule musique de film - celle du film d'Elia Kazan *Sur les quais* (1954) dans lequel joue le jeune Marlon Brando. Ce drame des docks de NewYork est un classique, ceci en grande partie grâce à la puissance de la musique de Bernstein. En 1955, Bernstein en tira une suite symphonique dont il dirigea la première, donnée par le Boston Symphony Orchestra le 11 août de la même année, àTanglewood. La suite incorpore adroitement tous les thèmes et toutes les textures du morceau original en un tout musical irrésistible qui est entièrement indépendant de l'élan visuel du film.

Prelude, Fugue and Riffs pour clarinette et ensemble de jazz fut joué pour la première fois en direct à la télévision le 16 octobre 1955 par Benny Goodman et son orchestre (en fait , l'œuvre avait été composée en 1949 sur une commande deWoody Herman, mais elle était restée dans les tiroirs, Herman ayant dissous son orchestre). Le titre annonce le mariage de la musique de concert et du jazz, la forme baroque de Prélude et Fugue étant complétée par une série de riffs (dans le langage du jazz, un riff est une figure mélodique répétée, courte). Le Prélude, joué par les cuivres et la Fugue par les saxophones, révèle l'influence de Stravinski (qui avait écrit son *Ebony Concerto* pourWoody Herman en 1946). La clarinette solo ne fait son entrée qu'au moment des riffs, qu'elle joue dans le style jazz le plus pur avec le soutien du piano puis de tout l'orchestre, qui reprend également les thèmes du Prélude et de la Fugue.

Dans le *Divertimento*, Bernstein copia sciemment le style irrévérencieux de *Candide.* Composé en 1980 pour le centenaire du Boston Symphony Orchestra, il se base sur un motif de deux notes B – C (si - do) ("B" pour Boston, "C" pour le centenaire, ou représentant 100 en chiffres romains). L'ouverture "Sennets etTuckets" (mots utilisés par Shakespeare qui veulent dire "fanfares") devait à l'origine constituer la totalité du morceau, mais Bernstein vit un tel potentiel dans cette ouverture qu'il écrivit huit courts mouvements, un pour chaque section de l'orchestre. Dans "Sennets etTuckets" le motif B – C est donné immédiatement par les cuivres, et fait allusion brièvement aux *Dumbarton Oaks* de Stravinski, une des nombreuses plaisanteries musicales du morceau. La valse (pour cordes) dans une mesure 7/8, est une douce parodie du style des salons viennois; la Mazurka (anches doubles et harpe) est une évocation de la musique de l'Europe de l'est; et la Samba donne un parfum latin inattendu. Le "Turkey Trot" rappelle l'atmosphère champêtre d'Aaron Copland. "Sphinxes" contient deux expositions d'une mélodie dodécaphonique ascendante, chacune finissant par une cadence diatonique banale – Mahler et Shostakovich semblent ici être les cibles visées. Le Blues pour cuivres et percussion est une des évocations du jazz les plus sophistiquées de Bernstein avec peut-être un salut au *Porgy and Bess* de Gershwin. Le finale, "In Memoriam" des anciens membres de l'orchestre, commence par un canon aux flûtes, puis se transforme en une marche tumultueuse, "The BSO Forever", qui rappelle *Stars and Stripes Forever* de Sousa et fait aussi référence à *La Marche de Radetski* de Johann Strauss.

Malcolm MacDonald

Vorwort

Bernsteins *Candide*, eine Operette frei nach Voltaires gleichnamigem satirischem Roman, wurde 1956 auf ein Libretto von Lillian Hellmann komponiert und am 1. Dezember am Martin-Beck-Theater in New York uraufgeführt. Anschließend bearbeitete der Komponist die Ouvertüre für großes Orchester und führte sie erstmals am 26. Januar 1957 mit dem New York Philharmonic Orchestra auf. Seitdem gehört die Ouvertüre zu den am häufigsten gespielten Werken Bernsteins. Hinter ihrer scheinbaren Schlichtheit verbergen sich witzige musikalische Anspielungen, die nur Eingeweihten verständlich sind. Nach der Eingangsfanfare läßt Bernstein kurz die beliebtesten Stücke dieser Operette Revue passieren. Das Duett „Oh Happy we" (Takt 83) stellt das lyrische zweite Thema vor, und die vor Leben sprühende Koda, die auf die Arie „Glitter and be Gay" anspielt, leitet das fröhlich-bunte Finale der Ouvertüre ein.

Überraschenderweise hat Bernstein nur ein einziges Mal für den Film komponiert, 1954 für *Die Faust im Nacken* von Elia Kazan. Die suggestive Musik Bernsteins hat wesentlich zum Erfolg dieses Klassikers mit dem jungen Marlon Brando beigetragen. 1955 stellte Bernstein aus der Filmmusik eine symphonische Suite her und leitete das Boston Symphony Orchestra bei der Uraufführung am 11. August in Tanglewood. Geschickt werden in der Suite Themen und musikalische Gestalten der Filmmusik zu einem fesselnden musikalischen Ganzen verbunden, völlig unabhängig von der visuellen Ebene des Films.

Obwohl bereits 1949 im Auftrag von Woody Herman komponiert, wurden *Präludium, Fuge und Riffs* für Klarinette und Jazz-Ensemble erstmals am 16. Oktober 1955 von Benny Goodman und seiner Band live im Fernsehen aufgeführt. Der Titel kündigt die Verbindung von klassischer Musik und Jazz an, bei der die barocken Formen von Präludium und Fuge durch mehrere Riffs (im Jazz eine kurze, oft wiederholte Melodiefigur) ergänzt werden. Das von den Blechläsern gespielte Präludium und die Fuge für Saxophone zeigen den Einfluß von Strawinsky, dessen *Ebony Concerto* (1946) ebenfalls für Woody Herman entstanden war. Die Soloklarinette setzt erst bei den Riffs ein, die sie in bestem Jazz-Stil mit Klavierbegleitung und danach mit der ganzen Band spielt, wobei die Band wieder Themen aus Präludium und Fuge aufnimmt.

Divertimento stellt einen bewußten Rückgriff Bernsteins auf den frechen Stil von *Candide* dar. Das Stück wurde 1980 zum hundertjährigen Bestehen des Boston Symphony Orchestra komponiert und basiert auf einem zweitönigen Motiv B-C („B" für Boston, „C" für 100 in römischen Ziffern). Der Eröffnungssatz „Sennets and Tuckets" (Shakespeare-Englisch für „Fanfaren") war ursprünglich als das einzige Stück vorgesehen, bis Bernstein die Möglichkeiten des Materials erkannte und acht kurze Sätze schrieb, die jeweils eine Instrumentengruppe des Orchesters besonders hervorheben. „Sennets and Tuckets" stellt das B-C-Motiv in den Blechbläsern vor und enthält einige Takte aus Strawinskys *Dumbarton Oaks*; nur einer der vielen musikalischen Scherze dieses Stückes. Der Walzer für Streicher im 7/8-Takt ist eine liebevolle Parodie auf Wiener Salonmusik, die Mazurka für Oboen, Fagotte und Harfe ein Anklang an osteuropäische Musik, und der Samba verleiht dem Ganzen ein unerwartetes südamerikanisches Flair. Der ländliche Turkey Trot („Putertrab") erinnert an Aaron Copland. In „Sphinxes" kommt zweimal eine ansteigende Zwölftonmelodie vor, die jeweils mit einer banalen diatonischen Kadenz endet: Mahler und Schostakowitsch lassen grüßen. Der Blues für Blechbläser und Schlagzeug ist raffiniertester Jazz und läßt an Gershwins *Porgy und Bess* denken. Das Finale, ein „In Memoriam" für ehemalige Orchestermitglieder, beginnt mit einem Kanon für Flöten und geht dann in einen lauten Marsch, „The BSO Forever", über, der an Sousas *Stars and Stripes Forever* erinnert und auch Anklänge an Johann Strauß' *Radetzky-Marsch* enthält.

Malcolm MacDonald

Overture to *Candide* : *Instrumentation*

Piccolo	Percussion:
2 Flutes	Timpani
2 Oboes	Snare Drum
Clarinet in E♭	Tenor Drum
2 Clarinets in B♭	Bass Drum
Bass Clarinet in B♭	Cymbals (Piatti)
2 Bassoons	Triangle
Contrabassoon	Glockenspiel
	Xylophone
4 Horns in F	
2 Trumpets in B♭	Harp
3 Trombones	
Tuba	Strings

Duration: circa 4 minutes

This overture to the comic operetta *Candide* (based on Voltaire's satire) had its first concert performance by the New York Philharmonic under the direction of the composer on 26 January 1957.

This printing incorporates changes to the orchestration made by the composer during the concert performances (and recording) of *Candide*, under his direction in London, in December 1989.

IMPORTANT NOTICE
The unauthorised copying of the whole or any part of this publication is illegal

OVERTURE TO "CANDIDE"

LEONARD BERNSTEIN

Allegro molto con brio 𝅗𝅥 = 132

Piccolo
Flutes 1 2
Oboes 1 2
Clarinet in E♭
Clarinets in B♭ 1 2
Bass Clarinet in B♭
Bassoons 1 2
Contrabassoon
Horns in F 1 2 3 4
Trumpets in B♭ 1 2
Trombones 1 2 3
Tuba
Timpani
Percussion
Harp
Violin I
Violin II
Viola
Violoncello
Contrabass

tr♮ ff a2 tr♯ a2 with hard sticks gliss. S.D. f pizz.

© Copyright 1955, 1957, 1958, 1976, 1982, 1990, 1994 by The Estate of Leonard Bernstein. Copyright Renewed
Leonard Bernstein Music Publishing Company LLC, Publisher
Boosey & Hawkes, Inc., Sole Agent.

Corrected Edition 1998

6
Picc.
tr
a2
Fl.
ff brillante
Ob.
ff
Cl. in E♭
Cl. in B♭
Bs.Cl.
dim.
mf
Bsn.
Cbn.
Hn. in F
f marc.
Tpt. in B♭
Tbn. 3
Tuba
(p)
S.D.
B.D.
Tri.
Perc.
pp
Harp
Vn. I
arco
f brillante
Vn. II
div.
arco
Vla.
ff martelé
Vc.
Cb.

12
Picc.
ff
a2
Fl.
a2
Ob.
Cl. in E♭
Cl. in B♭
Bs.Cl.
a2
Bsn.
Hn. in F
Harp
Vn.I
Vn.II
Vla.
Vc.
Cb.
12

17
Picc.
Fl.
Ob.
Cl. in E♭
Cl. in B♭
Bs.Cl.
Bsn.
Cbn.
Hn. in F
Tpt. in B♭
Tbn.
Tuba
Timp.
Perc.
Tri.
Xylo.
Vn. I
Vn. II
Vla.
Vc.
Cb.
a2
unis.
pizz.
tr
17

23
Picc.
Fl.
Ob.
Cl. in E♭
Cl. in B♭
Bs.Cl.
Bsn.
Cbn.
Hn. in F
Perc.
B.D.
Harp
Vn. I
Vn. II
Vla.
Vc.
Cb.
tr
a2
ff
mf
f
dim.
arco
div.
pizz.
23

29
Picc.
Fl.
Ob.
Cl. in E♭
Cl. in B♭
Bs.Cl.
Bsn.
Cbn.
Hn. in F
Tpt. in B♭
Tbn.
Tuba
Perc.
Harp
Vn. I
Vn. II
Vla.
Vc.
Cb.
a2
cresc.
ff
8va
f
gliss.
S.D.
B.D.
Cym.
(B♮, E♮, A♮)
unis.
29

35
loco
gliss.
Picc.
a2
Fl.
Ob.
Cl. in E♭
Cl. in B♭
Bs.Cl.
Bsn.
Cbn.
Hn. in F
Tpt. in B♭
1. mute
Tbn.
Tuba
S.D.
B.D.
Tri.
Cym.
Xylo.
Perc.
pizz.
Vn. I
Vn. II
Vla.
Vc.
Cb.
ff
f

41
Picc.
gliss.
ff
Fl.
a2
Ob.
Cl. in E♭
Cl. in B♭
B.Cl.
Bsn.
Cbn.
Hn. in F
open
(1.)
Tpt. in B♭
Tbn.
Tuba
f
Timp.
B.D.
Tri.
Perc.
Xylo.
Vn. I
arco
Vn. II
Vla.
Vc.
Cb.
pizz.
41

47
Picc.
Fl.
Ob.
Cl. in E♭
Cl. in B♭
B.Cl.
Bsn.
Cbn.
Hn. in F
Tpt. in B♭
Tbn.
Tuba
Timp.
f
Perc.
S.D.
Cym. (pair)
f
Vn. I
Vn. II
Vla.
pizz.
Vc.
(pizz.)
Cb.
47

54
Picc.
ff acuto
a2
Fl.
ff acuto
a2
Ob.
ff acuto
Cl. in E♭
ff acuto
a2
Cl. in B♭
ff acuto
Hn. in F
f
3.
f
1. mute
Tpt. in B♭
Tbn.
Tuba
Timp.
S.D.
Perc.
Tri.
p
Xylo.
f
pizz.
arco
Vn. I
ff
mf sub., dolce
pizz.
arco
Vn. II
ff
mf sub.
pizz.
arco
Vla.
ff
mf sub.
Vc.
Cb.
54

60
Fl.1
Perc.
Tri.
pp
Harp
Vn.I
Vn.II
Vla.
solo
mp
p
p
3
dim.
3
pp
3 sole
p
60
65
Fl. 1
Ob.
Cl. in B♭
Bs.Cl.
Bsn. 1
Perc.
Harp
Vla.
solo
mp
sfp
solo
p
p
p
solo
p
solo
p
Glsp.
p
p
65

70
Picc.
Fl. 1
Ob.
Cl. in E♭
Cl. in B♭
Bs.Cl.
Bsn. 1
Perc.
Vn. I
2 soli
Glsp.
dim.
76
tutte
pizz.
Vla.
Vc.

83
Cl. in E♭
Cl. 1 in B♭
mf cant.
Bs. Cl.
mf cant.
Bsn.
mp
mp
Cbn.
mp
div.
arco
Vla.
mf cant.
arco
Vc.
mp
arco
Cb. (div.)
mp
(pizz.)
mp
83
89
Cl. 1 in B♭
dim.
Bs. Cl.
dim.
Bsn.
Cbn.
Vla.
dim.
Vc.
Cb. (div.)
89

94
Ob.
1
2
mf cant.
mf cant.
Cl. in B♭
1
2
a2
6
mf cant.
Bs. Cl.
Bsn.
1
2
mf cant.
Cbn.
Harp
p gliss.
(A♮)
mf
tutti
Vn. I
mf cant.
Vn. II
mf cant.
unis.
Vla.
mf cant.
Vc.
Cb. (div.)
94

100
Ob.
Cl. in B♭
a2
Bs. Cl.
Bsn.
Cbn.
Harp
Vn. I
Vn. II
Vla.
Vc.
Cb. (div.)
dim.
100

106
Fl.
1
2
mf
f cant.
dim.
Ob.
Cl. in B♭
f
Bs. Cl.
Bsn.
Cbn.
Hn. in F
1
2
3
4
mf
Harp
B♭ major
gliss.
p
(A♮)
Vn. I
f espr.
Vn. II
Vla.
Vc.
Cb. (div.)
106

112
Fl.
1
2
f sub.
dim.
Ob.
Cl. in B♭
Bs. Cl.
Bsn.
a2
Hn. in F
mf sub.
Harp
mf dim.
Vn. I
Vn. II
Vla.
Vc.
Cb. (div.)
f sub.
112

118
Picc.
Fl.
Ob.
Cl. in E♭
Cl. in B♭
Bs. Cl.
a2
Bsn.
Hn. in F
Harp
Vn. I
Vn. II
Vla.
Vc.
Cb. (div.)
p
pp
p dolce
arco
118

123
Picc.
ff dolce
Fl.
ff dolce
Ob.
ff dolce
Cl. in E♭
ff dolce
Cl. in B♭
a2
ff dolce
Bs. Cl.
ff dolce
Bsn.
a2
ff dolce
Cbn.
f dolce
Hn. in F
a2
f espr. dolce
a2
f espr. dolce
Tpt. in B♭
open
f dolce
open
f dolce
Tbn.
f
f
Tuba
f dolce
Vn. I
ff dolce
Vn. II
ff dolce
Vla.
ff dolce
Vc.
ff dolce
Cb.
unis.
ff dolce
123

129
Picc.
Fl.
Ob.
Cl. in E♭
a2
Cl. in B♭
Bs. Cl.
a2
Bsn.
Cbn.
(a2)
Hn. in F
(a2)
Tpt. in B♭
Tbn.
Tuba
S.D.
Perc.
p cresc.
Vn. I
Vn. II
Vla.
Vc.
Cb.
cresc.
129

134
Picc.
Fl.
Ob.
Cl. in E♭
Cl. in B♭
Bs.Cl.
Bsn.
Cbn.
Hn. in F
Tpt. in B♭
Tbn.
Tuba
Timp.
Perc.
Harp
Vn. I
Vn. II
Vla.
Vc.
Cb.
a2
gliss.
S.D.
B.D.
Tri.
Cym.
pizz.

140
solo
Fl. 1
mp
Cl. in B♭ 1 2
mf
p
Bs. Cl.
p
Bsn. 1 2
p
Hn. in F 1 2 3 4
Harp
dim.
p
Vc.
p
Cb.
p
140
145
Picc.
p sempre
1.
Fl. 1 2
p
solo
Ob. 1
p
Cl. in B♭ 1 2
Bs. Cl.
pp
Bsn. 1 2
pp
Glsp.
Perc.
pp
Harp
1. solo
arco
Vn. I
p
div. pizz.
Vn. II
p
pizz.
Vla.
p
145

150
Picc.
Fl.
Ob.
Cl. in E♭
Cl. in B♭
Bs. Cl.
Bsn.
Cbn.
Hn. in F
Tpt. in B♭
Tbn.
Tuba
Perc.
Harp
Vn. I
Vn. II
Vla.
Vc.
Cb.
1.
a2
sub.
S.D.
B.D.
Cym.
Glsp.
(1. solo)
tutti
unis. arco
arco
150

155
Picc.
gliss.
gliss.
a2
Fl.
1
2
Ob.
Cl. in E♭
Cl. in B♭
Bs. Cl.
Bsn.
Cbn.
Hn. in F
1
2
3
4
Tpt. in B♭
1.
2.
Tbn.
Tuba
S.D.
B.D.
Cym.
Perc.
Harp
ff
Vn. I
Vn. II
Vla.
Vc.
Cb.
155

161
Picc.
Fl.
Ob.
Cl. in E♭
Cl. in B♭
B.Cl.
Bsn.
Cbn.
Hn. in F
Tpt. in B♭
Tbn.
Tuba
Timp.
Perc.
Cym. (pair)
S.D.
Harp
Vn. I
Vn. II
Vla.
Vc.
pizz.
Cb.
pizz.
161

168
Picc.
ff acuto
Fl.
a2
ff acuto
Ob.
a2
ff acuto
Cl. in E♭
ff acuto
Cl. in B♭
a2
ff acuto
Hn. in F
f
3.
f
Tpt. in B♭
1. mute
f
Tbn.
Tuba
Timp.
S.D.
Perc.
Tri.
p
Xylo.
f
Vn. I
pizz.
ff
arco
mf sub., dolce
Vn. II
pizz.
ff
arco
mf sub.
Vla.
pizz.
ff
arco
mf sub.
Vc.
Cb.
168

174
1.
2.
Fl.
1
2
Ob. 1
Cl. 1 in B♭
Bsn. 1
Hn. 1 in F
Perc.
Harp
Vn. I
Vn. II
Vla.
Vc.
Cb.
Tri.
pp
p
solo
p cant.
arco
179

184
Picc.
p cant.
Fl.
Ob.
p
Cl. in E♭
Cl. in B♭
p
Bs. Cl.
Bsn. 1
Cbn.
Hn. in F
p
Tpt. in B♭
Tbn.
Tuba
Timp.
Perc.
Harp
Vn. I
grazioso
Vn. II
Vla.
Vc.
Cb.
184

189
Picc.
Fl.
Ob.
Cl. in E♭
Cl. in B♭
Bs. Cl.
Bsn.
Cbn.
Hn. in F
Tpt. in B♭
Tbn.
Tuba
Timp.
Perc.
Harp
Vn. I
Vn. II
Vla.
Vc.
Cb.
cresc.
a2
1.
open
cant.
(soft sticks)
Cym. (pair)
gliss.
pizz.
189

194
Picc.
Fl.
Ob.
Cl. in E♭
Cl. in B♭
Bs. Cl.
Bsn.
Cbn.
Hn. in F
Tpt. in B♭
Tbn.
Tuba
Timp.
Perc.
Harp
Vn. I
Vn. II
Vla.
Vc.
Cb.
a2
(a2)
fff
dolce
dim.
Cym.
mf
gliss.
194

senza rall.
200
Picc.
Fl.
Ob. 1
Cl. in E♭
Cl. in B♭
Bs. Cl.
a2
Bsn.
Cbn.
Hn. in F
Tpt. 2 in B♭
Tbn.
Tuba
Timp.
Perc.
Harp
dim.
senza rall.
Vn. I
Vn. II
Vla.
Vc.
Cb.
200

206
G.P.
solo
Fl. 1
Ob. 1
Bsn.
Hn. in F
pp staccatissimo
Tri.
Cym.
Perc.
pizz.
Vn. II
Vla.
Vc.
213
Picc.
Cl. in B♭
Bs. Cl.
Timp.
hard sticks
Harp
Vn. I
arco
Cb.
p cresc. poco a poco
a2
nat.
(pizz.)

219
Picc.
Fl.
Ob.
Cl. in E♭
Cl. in B♭
Bs. Cl.
Bsn.
Cbn.
Hn. in F
Tpt. in B♭
Tbn.
Tuba
Timp.
Perc.
Harp
Vn. I
Vn. II
Vla.
Vc.
Cb.
cresc. molto
f sempre cresc.
f staccatissimo
mf staccatissimo
a2
1.
2.
8va
Tri.
Cym.
B.D.
arco

225
Picc.
(sempre cresc.)
a2 8va
loco
Fl.
a2
Ob.
Cl. in E♭
Cl. in B♭
Bs. Cl.
a2 (sempre cresc.)
Bsn.
Cbn.
Hn. in F
f
sempre cresc.
Tpt. in B♭
Tbn.
Tuba
Timp.
B.D.
Tri.
Cym.
Perc.
Harp
(8va)
Vn. I
Vn. II
Vla.
Vc.
Cb.
225

Più mosso (𝅗𝅥 = 152)
231
Picc.
Fl.
Ob.
Cl. in E♭
Cl. in B♭
Bs. Cl.
Bsn.
Cbn.
Hn. in F
Tpt. in B♭
Tbn.
Tuba
Timp.
Perc.
S.D.
T.D.
B.D.
Tri.
Cym.
Harp
Più mosso (𝅗𝅥 = 152)
(8va)
Vn. I
Vn. II
Vla.
Vc.
Cb.
pizz.
pizz.
a2
231

237
Picc.
p cresc.
Fl.
a2
cresc.
Ob.
p cresc.
Cl. in E♭
p cresc.
Cl. in B♭
p cresc.
Bs. Cl.
p cresc.
Bsn.
p cresc.
Cbn.
p cresc.
Hn. in F
cresc.
cresc.
Tpt. in B♭
cresc.
Tbn.
Tuba
Timp.
cresc.
S.D.
T.D.
Perc.
Glsp.
p cresc.
Harp
cresc.
Vn. I
cresc.
Vn. II
cresc.
Vla.
cresc.
Vc.
cresc.
Cb.
cresc.
237

243
Picc.
cresc. molto
f
cresc.
a2
Fl.
Ob.
Cl. in E♭
Cl. in B♭
Bs. Cl.
Bsn.
Cbn.
Hn. in F
Tpt. in B♭
Tbn.
Tuba
Timp.
S.D.
T.D.
Perc.
Glsp.
Harp
Vn. I
Vn. II
Vla.
Vc.
Cb.
243

249
Picc.
a2
Fl.
Ob.
Cl. in E♭
Cl. in B♭
Bs.Cl.
Bsn.
Cbn.
Hn. in F
Tpt. in B♭
Tbn.
Tuba
Timp.
S.D.
T.D.
Perc.
Glsp.
Harp
Vn. I
Vn. II
Vla.
Vc.
Cb.
249

255
Picc.
Fl.
Ob.
Cl. in E♭
Cl. in B♭
Bs. Cl.
Bsn.
Cbn.
Hn. in F
Tpt. in B♭
Tbn.
Tuba
Timp.
B.D.
Cym.
Glsp.
Perc.
Harp
Vn. I
Vn. II
Vla.
Vc.
Cb.
a2
1.
pizz.
arco
brillante
(pizz.)
255

261
Picc.
Fl.
a2
Ob.
a2
Cl. in B♭
Bs. Cl.
Bsn.
Cbn.
Hn. in F
Tpt. 1 in B♭
Tuba
Perc.
Glsp.
Vn. I
Vn. II
Vla.
Vc.
Cb.
arco
266
Cl. in E♭
Tri.
cresc.
cresc. molto

271
Picc.
Fl. 1 2
a2
Ob. 1 2
Cl. in E♭
Cl. in B♭ 1 2
Bs. Cl.
Bsn.
Cbn.
Hn. in F 1 2 3 4
Tpt. in B♭ 1 2
Tbn. 1 2 3
Tuba
Timp.
Perc.
B.D.
Tri.
Cym.
Harp
gliss.
Vn. I
Vn. II
Vla.
Vc.
Cb.
arco
fff
ff
271

277
Picc.
Fl. 1 2
a2
Ob. 1 2
a2
Cl. in E♭
Cl. in B♭ 1 2
Bs. Cl.
ff
Bsn. 1 2
a2
ff
Cbn.
ff
Hn. in F 1 2
fff cant.
3 4
fff cant.
Tpt. in B♭ 1 2
1.
Tbn. 1 2
fff cant.
3
Tuba
ff
Timp.
ff
Perc.
B.D.
Tri.
Cym.
Harp
Vn. I
Vn. II
Vla.
Vc.
Cb.
277

283
Picc.
Fl.
a2
Ob.
a2
Cl. in E♭
Cl. in B♭
a2
Bs.Cl.
Bsn.
a2
Cbn.
pp
ff
Hn. in F
Tpt. in B♭
Tbn.
Tuba
Timp.
Perc.
B.D.
Tri.
Cym.
Glsp.
f
Vn. I
div. pizz.
unis.
arco
p
Vn. II
Vla.
Vc.
Cb.
283

Symphonic Suite from *On the Waterfront* : *Instrumentation*

Piccolo
2 Flutes
2 Oboes
Clarinet in E♭
2 Clarinets in B♭
Bass Clarinet in B♭
Alto Saxophone in E♭
2 Bassoons
Contrabassoon

4 Horns in F
3 Trumpets in B♭
3 Trombones
Tuba

Percussion (3 or 4 players):
- Timpani
- Snare Drum
- Bass Drum
- 3 Tuned Drums
- 2 Tam-tams
- Cymbals
- Woodblock
- Triangle
- Glockenspiel
- Xylophone
- Vibraphone
- Chimes

Piano

Harp

Strings

Duration: circa 22 minutes

For my Son Alexander

ON THE WATERFRONT

SYMPHONIC SUITE FROM THE FILM

LEONARD BERNSTEIN (1955)

Andante (with dignity) ♩= 60

Piccolo
Flute 1. 2.
Oboe 1. 2.
Eb Clarinet
Clarinet in Bb 1. 2.
Bass Clarinet in Bb
Alto Saxophone in Eb
Bassoon 1. 2.
Contra Bassoon

Horn in F 1. 2. — 1. Solo — *mp* — *cresc.* — *f* — *mf dim.* — *dolce* — *p*
Horn in F 3. 4.

Trumpet in Bb 1. — (If too high for Horn) — *mp* — *cresc.* — *f* — *mf dim.* — *dolce* — *p*
Trumpet in Bb 2. 3.

Trombone 1. 2.
Trombone 3. Tuba

Timpani 1. 2.
Percussion

Piano Harp

Andante (with dignity) ♩= 60

Violin. I
Violin II
Viola
Violoncello
Contrabass

© Copyright 1955, 1962 by The Estate of Leonard Bernstein. Copyright Renewed
Leonard Bernstein Music Publishing Company LLC, Publisher
Boosey & Hawkes, Inc., Sole Agent.

1
semplice
Fl. 1. 2.
Hn. 1.
Tpt. 1.
con sord. dolce
Solo
Trb. 1.
cresc.
dim.
2
(if too high for trumpets)
Ob. 1. 2.
lontano
Cl. 1. 2.
B. Cl.
sub-tone
con sord.
Tpt.
Harp
rall.
Presto barbaro 𝅗𝅥 = 96
Ob. 1.
1. hard sticks
Timp. 1.
Piano
una corda
stacc.

44830

*If there are enough timpani available, it is preferable that these two notes (¹B♮ & B♭; ²G & F♯) be played on two separate drums.

5
Solo
A. Sax. (Eb)
fff crudely
Timp.
meno f
3 Dr.
Perc.
Cym.
choke
Piano
ff
pizz.
Vc.
Cb.
A. Sax.
Tpt. 2.
con sord.
pp
sffz
S. D.
Rim shot
mf

6
Picc.
a2
Fl. 1. 2.
a2
Ob. 1. 2.
Eb Cl.
a2
Cl. 1. 2.
Bsn. 1. 2.
con sord.
1.
Tpt.
2. 3.
1.
Timp.
2.
cresc.
cresc.
3 Dr.
cresc.
Perc.
Cym.
6
Vl. I.
Vl. II.
Vla.
arco
Vc.
(pizz.)
Cb.

7
Picc.
Fl. 1. 2.
a2
Ob. 1. 2.
mp
cresc.
Eb Cl.
Cl. 1. 2.
Bsn. 1. 2.
1. 2.
Hn.
3. 4.
p
1.
Tpt.
3.
con sord.
ff
1.
Timp.
2.
3 Dr.
Perc.
mp
Vl. I.
Vl. II.
Vla.
Vc.
arco
Cb.

Picc.
Fl. 1. 2.
a2
Ob. 1. 2.
a2
Cl. 1. 2.
a2
Bsn. 1. 2.
C. Bsn.
1. 2.
Hn.
3. 4.
1. 2.
Tpt.
3.
1. 2.
Trb.
3.
Perc.
3 Dr.
Vl. I.
Vl. II.
Vla.
Vc.
Cb.
f
p
dim.
poco a poco cresc.

Picc.
Fl. 1. 2.
a2
Ob. 1. 2.
Eb Cl.
Cl. 1. 2.
Bsn. 1. 2.
C.Bsn.
Hn. 1. 2.
3. 4.
Tpt. 1. 2.
3.
Trb. 1. 2.
3. Tuba
Timp.
Perc.
3 Dr.
Vl. I.
Vl. II.
Vla.
Vc.
Cb.
mp cresc.
mf
f
open
p cresc. molto
Tuba
tr
p cresc.
(mf)
cresc.
cresc. molto

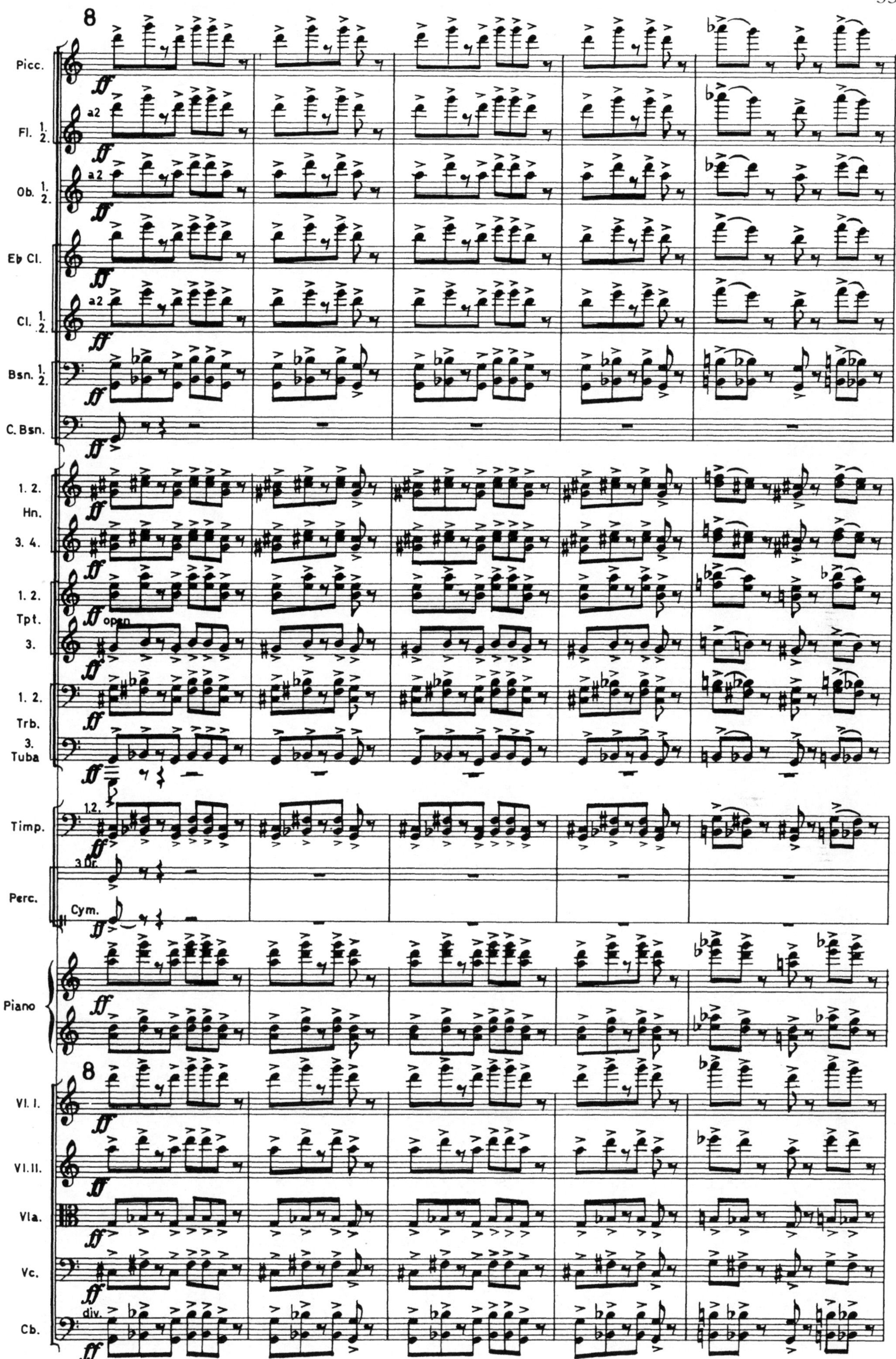
8
Picc.
Fl. 1. 2.
a2
Ob. 1. 2.
E♭ Cl.
Cl. 1. 2.
Bsn. 1. 2.
C. Bsn.
1. 2.
Hn.
3. 4.
1. 2.
Tpt.
open
3.
1. 2.
Trb.
3.
Tuba
1.2.
Timp.
3 Dr.
Perc.
Cym.
Piano
8
Vl. I.
Vl. II.
Vla.
Vc.
div.
Cb.

44830

9
Picc.
Fl. 1. 2.
a2
Ob. 1. 2.
Eb Cl.
Cl. 1. 2.
Bsn. 1. 2.
C. Bsn.
ff
fff
Hn. 1. 2.
3. 4.
Tpt. 1. 2.
3.
Trb. 1. 2.
3. Tuba
Timp.
1.2.
rimshots
S.D.
ord.
sub.
Xyl.
Perc.
Piano
Vl. I.
Vl. II.
Vla.
Vc.
Cb.
sffz-p

Picc.
Fl. 1. 2.
a 2
Ob. 1. 2.
Eb Cl.
Cl. 1. 2.
fff
S. D.
mp
Perc.
Xyl.
ff
Vl. I.
Vl. II.
sffz-p
sim.
Hn. 1. 2.
Hn. 3. 4.
Tpt. 1. 2.
pp
Timp.
1. marc.
1. 2.
cresc.
sffz p

(dura come 3/2)
long
flutt.
Picc.
cresc. molto
a2
Fl. 1. 2.
Ob. 1. 2.
Eb Cl.
f cresc. molto
Cl. 1. 2.
Bsn. 1. 2.
1. 2.
Hn.
3. 4.
f cresc.
Tpt.
3.
cresc.
Timp.
mf cresc.
S.D.
Perc.
Cym.
ff
p cresc.
Vl. I.
Vl. II.
Vla.
Vc.
Cb.

Adagio ♩= 76
10
Picc.
Fl. 1. 2.
Ob. 1. 2.
Eb Cl.
Cl. 1. 2.
Bsn. 1. 2.
C. Bsn.
1. 2.
Hn.
3. 4.
1. 2.
Tpt.
3.
1. 2.
Trb.
3.
Tuba
Timp.
Perc.
Cym.
S. D.
Xyl.
Adagio ♩= 76
10
Vl. I.
Vl. II.
Vla.
Vc.
Cb.
sul pont.
div.
unis.
cresc.
a2

Allegro molto agitato ♩= 152
Picc.
Fl. 1. 2.
Ob. 1. 2.
Eb Cl.
Cl. 1. 2.
Bsn. 1. 2.
C. Bsn.
1. 2. Hn. 3. 4.
1. 2. Tpt. 3.
1. 2. Trb. 3. Tuba
Timp.
Perc.
S.D.
1. con sord.
smorzando
non div.
unis.
nat.
div.
nat. unis.
Vl. I.
Vl. II.
Vla.
Vc.
Cb.

Fl. 1. 2.
a2 marc.
mf
f
Ob. 1. 2.
marc.
mf
f
Cl. 1. 2.
1.
cresc.
2.
p cresc.
mf cresc.
Bsn. 1. 2.
1. 2.
Hn.
3. 4.
mf
3.
f
1. 2.
Tpt.
3.
1.
dim. a niente
senza sord.
con sord.
mp
senza sord.
1. 2.
Trb.
3.
con sord.
mf
Timp.
Perc.
Cym.
Vl. I.
Vl. II.
Vla.
cresc.
mf cresc.
div.
Vc.
p cresc.
mf cresc.
Cb.

11
a2
Fl. 1. 2.
Ob. 1. 2.
1.
Cl. 1. 2.
2.
f
Bsn. 1. 2.
2.
f
1. 2.
Hn.
3.
3. 4.
1. 2.
Tpt.
f
if too high for horns
3.
f
1. 2.
Trb.
3.
1.
Timp.
f
11
Vl. I.
Vl. II.
f
Vla.
f
Vc.
f
Cb.

Fl. 1. 2.
a2
Ob. 1. 2.
Cl. 1. 2.
1.
2.
1.
cresc.
Bsn. 1. 2.
cresc.
Hn. 1. 2.
3. 4.
3.
Tpt. 1. 2.
3.
Trb. 1. 2.
3.
ff
Timp.
1.
Vl. I.
Vl. II.
Vla.
Vc.
Cb.

Picc.
Fl. 1. 2.
Ob. 1. 2.
E♭ Cl.
Cl. 1. 2.
Bsn. 1. 2.
1. 2. Tpt. 3.
1. 2. Trb. 3.
Timp.
Piano
ff marc.
Vl. I.
Vl. II.
Vla.
Vc.
Cb.

Picc.
Fl. 1. 2.
Ob. 1. 2.
Eb Cl.
Cl. 1. 2.
Bsn. 1. 2.
1. 2.
Tpt.
3.
1. 2.
Trb.
3.
Perc.
Cym.
Piano
Vl. I.
Vl. II.
Vla.
Vc.
Cb.

12
Picc.
Fl. 1. 2.
Ob. 1. 2.
a2
Eb Cl.
Cl. 1. 2.
a2
Bsn. 1. 2.
a2
1. 2.
Hn.
3. 4.
1. 2.
Tpt.
3.
1. 2.
Trb.
3.
1. 2.
Timp.
Perc.
B.D.
Piano
12
détaché
sim.
Vl. I.
Vl. II.
div.
Vla.
unis.
Vc.
Cb.

Fl. 1. 2.
Ob. 1. 2.
a2
Cl. 1. 2.
Bsn. 1. 2.
Hn. 3. 4.
Perc.
B.D.
Piano
Vl. I.
Vl. II.
Vla.
Vc.
con sord.
Tpt. 1. 2.
mf
(non cresc.)
Wd. Bl.

13
Fl. 1. 2.
a2
Ob. 1. 2.
Cl. 1. 2.
a2
Bsn. 1. 2.
open
ff
open
ff
1. 2.
Hn.
3. 4.
1. 2.
Tpt.
3.
1. 2.
Trb.
3.
Perc.
B. D.
f
Piano
13
Vl. I.
Vl. II.
Vla.
Vc.
Cb.

44830

Picc.
Fl. 1. 2.
Ob. 1. 2.
a2
Eb Cl.
Cl. 1. 2.
Bsn. 1. 2.
1. 2.
Hn.
3. 4.
1. 2.
Tpt.
3.
senza sord.
1. 2.
Trb.
3.
Timp.
Perc.
Wd. Bl.
Piano
Vl. I.
Vl. II.
Vla.
unis.
Vc.
div.
Cb.
div.

Picc.
8
Fl. 1. 2.
Ob. 1. 2.
Eb Cl.
Cl. 1. 2.
1.
2.
1.
Bsn. 1. 2.
1.
2.
1.
C. Bsn.
fff
1. 2.
Tpt.
3.
1. 2.
Trb.
3.
Timp.
Vl. I.
Vl. II.
sim.
Vla.
sim.
Vc.
sim.
Cb.
sim.

Picc.
Fl. 1. 2.
Ob. 1. 2.
Eb Cl.
Cl. 1. 2.
Bsn. 1. 2.
C. Bsn.
1. 2. Tpt. 3.
1. 2. Trb. 3.
Timp.
Vl. I.
Vl. II.
Vla.
Vc.
Cb.

14
Picc.
sffz p
fff
Fl. 1. 2.
Ob. 1. 2.
sffz p
fff
Eb Cl.
sffz p
fff
Cl. 1. 2.
1.
a2
Bsn. 1. 2.
1.
a2
1. 2.
Tpt.
3.
sffz
fff
1. 2.
Trb.
3.
sffz
fff
Perc.
Cym.
ff
Wd. Bl.
ff
Piano
fff
14
Vl. I.
Vl. II.
Vla.
Vc.
Cb.

Picc.
Fl. 1. 2.
a2
Ob. 1. 2.
a2
Eb Cl.
Cl. 1. 2.
a2
Bsn. 1. 2.
a2
C. Bsn.
1. 2.
Hn.
3. 4.
a2
ff
1. 2.
Tpt.
3.
1. 2.
Trb.
3.
Tuba
Timp.
ff
Chimes
Perc.
fff
Vl. I.
Vl. II.
Vla.
Vc.
unis.
Cb.
unis.

15 Alla breve (Poco più mosso) 𝅗𝅥 = 88
Tpt. 1. 2.
f nobile
Trb. 1.
f nobile
15 Alla breve (Poco più mosso) 𝅗𝅥 = 88
Vl. I.
Vl. II.
Vla.
Vc.
Cb.
un poco accel.
1. 2.
Tpt.
3.
cresc.
f cresc.
ff
1. 2.
Trb.
3.
f cresc.
ff
Perc.
Cym.
mf cresc.
un poco accel.
Vl. I.
Vl. II.
Vla.
div.
Vc.
Cb.

al
Presto come prima 𝅗𝅥 = 96
Picc.
Fl. 1. 2.
Ob. 1. 2.
Eb Cl.
Cl. 1. 2.
Bsn. 1. 2.
C. Bsn.
Hn. 1. 2.
3. 4.
Tpt. 1. 2.
3.
Trb. 1. 2.
3.
Tuba
Timp.
Perc.
Cym
f cresc.
Vl. I.
Vl. II.
Vla.
Vc.
Cb.
a2
unis.
div.

Picc.
a2
Fl. 1. 2.
a2
Ob. 1. 2.
E♭ Cl.
a2
Cl. 1. 2.
Bsn. 1. 2.
C. Bsn.
1. 2.
Hn.
3. 4.
1. 2.
Tpt.
3.
1. 2.
Trb.
a2
3.
Tuba
1.2.
Timp.
Perc.
S. D. rimshots
ff
Vl. I.
Vl. II.
Vla.
Vc.
Cb.

16
Picc.
a2
Fl. 1. 2.
Ob. 1. 2.
Eb Cl.
Cl. 1. 2.
Bsn. 1. 2.
C. Bsn.
1. 2.
Hn.
3. 4.
1. 2.
Tpt.
3.
1. 2.
Trb.
3.
Tuba
1.2.
Timp.
S.D.
ord.
sub.
mp
Perc.
Xyl.
ff
16
Vl. I.
sffz-p
Vl. II.
Vla.
Vc.
Cb.

Picc.
Fl. 1. 2.
a2
Ob. 1. 2.
E♭ Cl.
Cl. 1. 2.
S.D.
Perc.
Xyl.
Vl. I.
sim.
Vl. II.
sim.
Picc.
Fl. 1. 2.
a2
Ob. 1. 2.
sffz-p
cresc.
Cl. 1. 2.
sffz-p
cresc.
1. 2.
Hn.
3. 4.
ff
Tpt. 1. 2.
pp
cresc.
1. marc.
1.2.
Timp.
mp
(mp) cresc.
mf cresc.
S.D.
Perc.
Xyl.
cresc.
mf cresc.
Vl. I.
sim.
cresc.
Vl. II.
sim.
cresc.

long (dura come 3/2)
flutt.
Picc.
cresc. molto
a2
Fl. 1. 2.
Ob. 1. 2.
Eb Cl.
cresc. molto
Cl. 1. 2.
Bsn. 1. 2.
long
1. 2.
Hn.
3. 4.
cresc.
Tpt.
3.
1. 2.
Timp.
Cym.
Perc.
S.D.
Vl. I.
Vl. II.
Vla.
Vc.
Cb.

Andante largamente ♩= 60
17
Picc.
Fl. 1. 2.
Ob. 1. 2.
Eb Cl.
Cl. 1. 2.
A. Sax.
Bsn. 1. 2.
C. Bsn.
1. 2.
Hn.
3. 4.
1. 2.
Tpt.
3.
1. 2.
Trb.
3.
Tuba
Timp.
Perc.
Cym.
S.D.
Xyl.
Chimes
espr.
non div.
unis.
with intensity
Vl. I.
Vl. II.
Vla.
Vc.
Cb.

Fl. 1. 2.
Ob. 1. 2.
Cl. 1. 2.
Bsn. 1. 2.
1. 2.
Hn.
3. 4.
1. soft stick
Timp.
Large Tam-tam
Perc.
Piano
Vl. I.
Vl. II.
Vla.
Vc.
Cb.
sim.
cresc.
mp cresc. molto
p cresc. molto

18
a2
Fl. 1. 2.
Ob. 1. 2.
Cl. 1. 2.
Bsn. 1. 2.
C. Bsn.
1. 2.
Hn.
3. 4.
Timp.
Perc.
Tam - tam
Piano
18
div.
Vl. I.
Vl. II.
Vla.
unis.
Vc.
Cb.

19
More flowing ♩= 72
Fl. 1. 2.
Ob. 1. 2.
Cl. 1. 2.
A. Sax.
lontano
Bsn. 1. 2.
a2
1. Solo
con sord.
1. 2.
Hn.
3. 4.
Timp.
Tam-tam
Perc.
Piano
Vl. I.
Vl. II.
Vla.
Vc.
Cb.
con sord.
div. a 3
senza espr.
dim.
19
More flowing ♩= 72

20 Still more flowing ♩ = 104
Solo
1.
espr.
Fl. 1. 2.
pp
mp
Cl. 1. 2.
p
a2
sub-tone
B. Cl.
p
Hn 1
poco f
pp
Harp
pp
20 Still more flowing ♩ = 104
Vl. I.
poco tenuto
a tempo
Fl. 1.
Cl. 1. 2.
B. Cl.
Harp
Fl. 1.
cresc.
Cl. 1. 2.
cresc.
B. Cl.
cresc.
Harp
cresc.

21
Fl. 1.
Cl. 1. 2.
B. Cl.
Harp
(♮)
f
dim.
p
pp
mf
21
(con sord.)
unis.
Vl. I.
Vl. II.
con sord.
Vla.
con sord.
Vc.
con sord.
unis.
Solo
espr.
mp
espr.

poco rall.
22 Poco meno mosso
Fl. 1.
cresc.
dim.
pp
Cl. 1. 2.
cresc.
dim. molto
pp
B. Cl.
cresc.
dim. molto
pp
Harp
cresc.
dim. molto
pp
poco rall.
22 Poco meno mosso
Vl. I.
cresc.
dim. molto
pp
Vl. II.
cresc.
mf
dim. molto
pp
Vla.
cresc.
mf
Vc.
div.
cresc.
mf cresc.
Cb.
poco tenuto
rall.
23 Lento ♩= 69
(non cresc.)
Perc.
Trgl.
ppp
poco tenuto
rall.
23 Lento ♩= 69
(con sord.)
div.
44830

Solo
Piano
mp
stacc.
una corda
sim.
mf
f
Vl. I.
p
f
mp
Vl. II.
Vla.
pizz.
Vc.
Cb.
24
1. Solo
Fl. 1. 2.
Cl. 1. 2.
poco a poco senza sord.
1. Sola senza sord.
mp espr.

Picc.
Fl. 1.
Cl. 1.
1. 2.
Tpt.
3.
Harp
Vl. I.
Vl. II.
Vla.
Vc.
pp
con sord.
con sord.
div. senza sord.
Tutti
senza sord.
mp
25 Moving forward ♩= 88, with warmth
Harp.
Cb.
unis. senza sord.
p
half
sim.

26
Harp
cresc.
mf
26
Vl. I.
cresc.
mf
Vl. II.
cresc.
mf
sempre cantabile
Vla.
cresc.
mf
sempre cantabile
Vc.
cresc.
mf
Tutti
Cb.
cresc.
mf
Harp
cresc.
Vl. I.
cresc.
Vl. II.
cresc.
Vla.
cresc.
Vc.
cresc.
Cb.
cresc.

27
a2
Bsn. 1. 2.
C. Bsn.
Hn. 1. 2.
senza sord.
Solo
Tpt. 1.
dolce cantabile
Harp
27
sempre espr.
Vl. I.
Vl. II.
Vla.
unis.
Vc.
div.
Cb.
cresc.

28 Largamente
Picc.
Fl. 1. 2.
Ob. 1. 2.
Cl. 1. 2.
B. Cl.
Bsn. 1. 2.
C. Bsn.
Hn. 1. 2.
Hn. 3. 4.
Tpt. 1.
Tpt. 2.
senza sord.
Trb. 1. 2.
3. Tuba
Harp
28 Largamente
Vl. I.
Vl. II.
Vla.
Vc.
Cb.
unis.

rall.
29
a tempo
Picc.
Fl. 1. 2.
Ob. 1. 2.
Cl. 1. 2.
B. Cl.
Bsn. 1. 2.
C. Bsn.
a2
cresc.
fff
ppp sub.
pp sub.
1. Solo
senza espr.
p
1. 2.
Hn.
3. 4.
Tpt.
3.
Trb.
3.
Tuba
con sord.
pp
ff
pp sub.
Susp. Cym.
Perc.
Vibraphone
Harp
Vl. I.
Vl. II.
Vla.
Vc.
Cb.
div.
pizz.
arco
pizz

poco rall.
Calmato
rit.
30 a tempo
Picc.
Fl. 1. 2.
Ob. 1. 2.
Cl. 1. 2.
Bsn. 1. 2.
1. 2.
Tpt.
3.
Trb. 1. 2.
Cym.
Perc.
Vib.
dim.
Harp
harm.
Vl. I.
Vl. II.
Vla.
Vc.
Cb.
unis.
arco
p dolce
dim.
pp

*a cut may be made from this bar to * (2 after 33)

33
Tpt. 1. 2.
Trb. 1.
33
Vl. I.
Vl. II.
Vla.
Vc.
Ancora più mosso ♩= 96
Picc.
Fl. 1. 2.
Ob. 1. 2.
Cl. 1. 2.
B. Cl.
Bsn. 1. 2.
C. Bsn
Tpt. 3.
con sord.
Ancora più mosso ♩= 96
Vl. I.
Vl. II.
Vla.
Vc.
Cb.
div.
trem.

stringendo
sempre string. . . . . . al
Picc.
a2
Fl. 1. 2.
Ob. 1. 2.
Cl. 1. 2.
B. Cl.
Bsn. 1. 2.
C. Bsn.
1. 2.
Hn.
3. 4.
cresc.
1. 2.
Tpt.
3.
senza sord.
pp cresc.
Perc.
S. D.
pp cresc. molto
stringendo
sempre string. . . . . . al
Vl. I.
mf sub.
f cresc. . . . molto
Vl. II.
unis.
Vla.
div.
Vc.
Cb.

34 Allegro non troppo, molto marcato ♩. = 108
Picc.
Fl. 1. 2.
Ob. 1. 2.
E♭ Cl.
Cl. 1. 2.
B. Cl.
Bsn. 1. 2.
C. Bsn.
Hn. 1. 2.
3. 4.
Tpt. 1. 2.
3.
Trb. 1. 2.
3. Tuba
Timp.
Perc.
S.D.
Chimes
Vl. I.
Vl. II.
Vla.
Vc.
Cb.
unis.
a 2
1.2.

35
Picc.
Fl. 1. 2.
Ob. 1. 2.
Eb Cl.
Cl. 1. 2.
B. Cl.
Bsn. 1. 2.
C. Bsn.
1. 2. Hn. 3. 4.
1. 2. Tpt. 3.
1. 2. Trb. 3. Tuba
Timp.
S.D.
Chimes
Perc.
35
Vl. I.
Vl. II.
Vla.
Vc.
Cb.
a2
div.
spicc.
unis.

Picc.
Fl. 1. 2.
a 2
Ob. 1. 2.
Eb Cl.
Cl. 1. 2.
B. Cl.
Bsn. 1. 2.
C. Bsn.
1. 2.
Hn.
3. 4.
Tpt.
3.
Trb.
3. Tuba
fff
Timp.
1. 2.
S. D.
ff
Cym.
Chimes
Xyl.
Perc.
Vl. I.
Vl. II.
unis.
Vla.
Vc.
Cb.

36
Picc.
Fl. 1. 2.
Ob. 1. 2.
Eb Cl.
Cl. 1. 2.
B. Cl.
Bsn. 1. 2.
C. Bsn.
1. 2. Hn. 3. 4.
1. 2. Tpt. 3.
1. 2. Trb.
3. Tuba
Timp.
Perc.
Cym.
Chimes
Xyl.
a2
unis.
div.
fff
ff
dim.
(Vlni. 1.2. verso il ponticello)
Vl. I.
Vl. II.
Vla.
Vc.
Cb.

Picc.
Fl.
Ob.
Cl.
B. Cl.
Bsn.
Hn.
Tpt.
Trb.
Perc.
Trgl.
Xyl.
Vl. I.
Vl. II.
Vla.
sul pont.
div.
pizz.
mf dim.
mp
a2

37
Picc.
Fl. 1. 2.
Ob. 1. 2.
Cl. 1. 2.
B.Cl.
Bsn. 1. 2.
1. 2.
Hn.
3. 4.
1. 2.
Tpt.
3.
1. 2.
Trb.
3.
Perc.
Xyl.
S.D.
Vl. I.
Vl. II.
Vla.
Vc.
Cb.
p
p sub.
ff sub.
ff
a2
ord.
pizz.

38
Picc.
Fl. 1. 2.
Ob. 1. 2.
dim. molto
Cl. 1. 2.
1. Solo
B. Cl.
Bsn. 1. 2.
Solo
Hn. 1. 2.
Hn. 3. 4.
a2
Tpt. 1. 2.
Tpt. 3.
Trb. 1. 2.
Trb. 3.
Perc.
S. D.
Xyl.
Vl. I.
unis.
Vl. II.
unis. arco
Vla.
Vc.
Cb.

Picc.
Fl. 1.
Timp.
Perc.
Xyl.
Chimes
pesante
Vl. I.
Vl. II.
Vla.
Vc.
Cb.
div.
dim.
39 Poco più sostenuto ♩= 92
Bsn. 1. 2.
Soli
espr.
con sord.
a2
1. 2. Hn. 3. 4.
1. 2. Trb.
3. Tuba
dim. sub.
muffled 1. 2.
pizz.
unis. pizz.

moving forward
♩= 108
Picc.
Fl. I.
Cl. 1. 2.
Bsn. 1. 2.
cresc.
mf
p
Xyl.
Perc.
mp
Harp
40
♩=♩(𝅗𝅥=54)
Picc.
ppp
Fl. 1. 2.
pp
Cl. 1. 2.
B. Cl.
A. Sax.
Solo subtone
Bsn. 1. 2.
Harp

rall.
Meno mosso
Picc.
dim. a niente
(if too difficult for oboes PPPP)
Fl. 1. 2.
pppp
Ob. 1. 2.
pppp
Cl. 1. 2.
1.
dim. a niente
B. Cl.
A. Sax.
Bsn. 1. 2.
1.
ppp
dim. a niente
più rall.
41
a tempo 𝅗𝅥 = 54
Picc.
Fl. 1. 2.
Ob. 1. 2.
Cl. 1. 2.
1.
Bsn. 1. 2.
1.
Susp. Cym.
ppp
(one player if desired)
Small Tam-tam
Large Tam-tam
ppp
Perc.
Vibraphone
p
Harp
p
più rall.
41
a tempo 𝅗𝅥 = 54
con sord.
Vl. I.
ppp
con sord.
Vl. II.
ppp
con sord.
Vla.
ppp
div. pizz.
Vc.
ppp
div. pizz.
Cb.
ppp

42
Picc.
Fl. 1. 2.
Ob. 1. 2.
Cl. 1. 2.
Bsn. 1. 2.
pp
p cresc.
cresc.
1. 2.
Tpt.
3.
con sord.
pp
p
1. 2.
Trb.
3.
con sord.
pp
poco cresc.
Cym.
T. tams
Vib.
Perc.
poco cresc.
mp cresc.
Harp
p
Vl. I.
Vl. II.
Vla.
Vc.
Cb.
unis.
poco cresc.
pp

43
Picc.
Fl. 1. 2.
Ob. 1. 2.
Eb Cl.
Cl. 1. 2.
B. Cl.
Bsn. 1. 2.
C. Bsn.
Hn. 1. 2.
3. 4.
Tpt. 1. 2.
3.
Trb. 1. 2.
3.
Timp.
Perc.
Cym.
T. tams.
Glock.
Harp
Vl. I.
Vl. II.
Vla.
Vc.
Cb.
mf cresc.
f
a2
senza sord.
2. con sord.
via sord.
p
mp cresc.
cresc.
mf
1.
2.

rall.
Picc.
Fl. 1. 2.
a2
Ob. 1. 2.
Eb Cl.
Cl. 1. 2.
B. Cl.
Bsn. 1. 2.
C. Bsn.
1. 2.
Hn.
3. 4.
open
1. 2.
Tpt.
3.
1. 2.
Trb.
3.
Tuba
molto
Timp.
cresc.
Cym.
T. tams
Perc.
Glock.
Harp
Vl. I.
Vl. II.
Vla.
Vc.
Cb.

44
rall.
Fl. 1. 2.
Ob. 1. 2.
Cl. 1. 2.
Bsn. 1. 2.
Very broadly
a2
Hn. 1. 2.
3. 4.
tutta forza
to the fore
Tpt. 1.
2.
3.
Trb. 1. 2.
3. Tuba
Perc.
Cym.
B.D.
Vl. I.
Vl. II.
Vla.
Vc.
Cb.

45 a tempo
Picc.
Fl. 1. 2.
Ob. 1. 2.
Eb Cl.
Cl. 1. 2.
B. Cl.
Bsn. 1. 2.
C. Bsn.
1. 2. Hn. 3. 4.
1. Tpt. 2. 3.
1. 2. Trb. 3. Tuba
Timp.
Cym.
Perc.
T. tams.
Piano
45 a tempo
Vl. I.
Vl. II.
Vla.
Vc.
arco
Cb.
arco

46
Picc.
Fl. 1. 2.
a2
Ob. 1. 2.
Eb Cl.
Cl. 1. 2.
B. Cl.
Bsn. 1. 2.
C. Bsn.
1. 2.
Hn.
3. 4.
bells up
p
1.
Tpt.
2. 3.
1. 2.
Trb.
3.
Tuba
Timp.
Cym.
Perc.
T.-tams
B. D.
fff
Piano
Vl. I.
full bows
Vl. II.
Vla.
Vc.
Cb.
div.

LEONARD BERNSTEIN
PRELUDE, FUGUE & RIFFS

Prelude, Fugue and Riffs : Instrumentation

Solo B♭ Clarinet*

1st E♭ Alto Saxophone (alternating
with B♭ Clarinet)
2nd E♭ Alto Saxophone
1st B♭ Tenor Saxophone
2nd B♭ Tenor Saxophone
E♭ Baritone Saxophone

1st B♭ Trumpet
2nd B♭ Trumpet
3rd B♭ Trumpet
4th B♭ Trumpet
5th B♭ Trumpet

1st Trombone
2nd Trombone
3rd Trombone
Bass Trombone (4th Trombone)

Piano

Percussion (2 players)
4 Tom-toms
Traps: Hi-Hat, Snare Drum, Bass
Drum, &c
Xylophone
Vibraphone
Woodblock
2 Timpani tuned

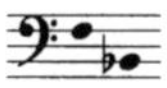

String bass (solo)

*The composer has suggested that the solo clarinet be discreetly amplified in performance.

To Benny Goodman

Prelude, Fugue and Riffs

for Solo Clarinet and Jazz Ensemble

Duration: ca. 9 minutes

Leonard Bernstein

Prelude

for the Brass

© Copyright 1950, 1978 by The Estate of Leonard Bernstein. Copyright Renewed
Leonard Bernstein Music Publishing Company LLC, Publisher
Boosey & Hawkes, Inc., Sole Agent.

Corrected Edition 1991

20
Bb Tpt.
mute off
(open)
Tbn.
B. Dr.
Perc.
(pizz.)
Bass
p cresc.
mf cresc. molto
2 Ton Toms
cresc.
mf cresc.

♪=♪(but with a bit more drag)
𝅗𝅥 = 80 ⟶ 𝅗𝅥 = 66
30
Bb Tpt.
fff
Tbn.
ff
gliss.
solid
Hi-Hat
ff slow drag
etc. ad lib. (very slow rock)
Perc.
B. Dr.
ff slow drag
etc. ad lib. (very slow rock)
Bass
40
mf
(ad lib.)
(ad lib.)

B♭ Tpt.
Tbn.
Perc.
Bass
Harmon mute
Harmon mute
(ff)
p sub.
mp
(ad lib.)
poco a poco accel. (to achieve opening beat ♩ = 160)
(in 4)
cresc.
mp cresc.
sim.

50
accel.
Bb Tpt.
mf
f cresc.
ff
f
cresc.
mf
mf cresc.
Tbn.
Perc.
Sn. Dr.
p
Bass
Original beat ♩= 160
60
(open)
as before
mp
mutes off
(mutes off)
B. Dr.
ff

Bb Tpt.
mf
p cresc.
mf cresc. molto
ff
open
Tbn.
Tom-Toms
cresc.
B. Dr.
Perc.
Bass
mf cresc.
70
G. P.
80
(in tempo)
fff
sff
Cym.
attacca
subito

Fugue
for the Saxes

100

Eb A. Sax. 1, 2

Bb T. Sax. 1, 2

Eb Bar. Sax.

p f p f p ff p

110

p dolce sim. p

cresc. f p sub. mf p espressivo

120

cresc. f p pp mf pp

Eb A. Sax.
Bb T. Sax.
Eb Bar. Sax.
sempre pp
pp ma espress.
130
p cresc.
mf
cresc.
p
mf cresc.
p legatissimo
140
ff
p relaxed
p staccatissimo

150

E♭ A. Sax. 1, 2
(non cresc.)
dim.
p easy
pp
B♭ T. Sax. 1, 2
sim.
dim.
E♭ Bar. Sax.
sim.
dim.

Riffs
for Everyone

♪ = ♪

E♭ Alto Saxophone 1, 2
B♭ Tenor Saxophone 1, 2
E♭ Baritone Saxophone
f
Piano Solo (miked)
f p f p f

B♭ Cl. Solo*
p lightly
poco
160
Pno
p sim.

B♭ Cl. Solo
mf
Pno.
p lightly
sim.

B♭ Cl. Solo
gliss.
170
Pno.
mf
Bass
pizz.
f

* The composer has suggested that the solo clarinet by discreetly amplified in performance.

B♭ Cl. Solo
Pno
Bass
mf
mp
sim.
cresc.
gliss.
f
(f)
f sempre
Perc.
Traps ad lib., accompaniment (brushes)
180
Pno.
Traps
ff
p
Xyl.
sim.
* + = slap, 0 = pluck.

190
mutes
Tbn.
Pno.
Xyl.
Perc.
Traps
Bass
B♭ Cl. Solo
E♭ A. Sax.
B♭ T. Sax.
E♭ Bar. Sax.
(to Vibraphone)
Vib.
(pizz.)
sim.

B♭ Cl. Solo
E♭ A. Sax.
change to B♭ Cl.
B♭ T. Sax.
E♭ Bar. Sax.
Pno.
ff
Vib.
Perc.
Traps
Bass
200
B♭ Cl. 1
B♭ Tpt. 1
mute off
Tbn.
f
W. Bl.
mp
Cym.

Bb Cl. Solo
Eb Bar. Sax.
Bb Tpt. 1
Tbn. 1
Pno.
Perc.
rip
Xyl.
W. Bl.
Cym.
cresc. sempre
210
Bb Tpt.
mute
mutes
(mute)
(mutes)
p sub.
(no Ped.)
arco,sul pont.
Bass

B♭ Cl. Solo
B♭ Cl. 1
E♭ A. Sax. 2
B♭ T. Sax. 1
2
E♭ Bar. Sax.
B♭ Tpt. 1
2
3
4
5
Tbn. 1
2
3
4
Pno.
Perc.
Vib.
Bass
p
cresc.
mp
pizz.
arco, sul pont.
8

220
Bb Cl. Solo
Bb Cl. 1
Eb A. Sax.2
Bb T. Sax.
Eb Bar. Sax.
Bb Tpt.
Tbn.
Pno.
Perc.
Vib.
Bass
mf cresc.
f
(open)
sim.

Bb Cl. Solo
Bb Cl. 1
Eb A. Sax. 2
Bb T. Sax. 1
2
Eb Bar. Sax.
1
2
Bb Tpt. 3
4
5
Tbn. 1
2
3
4
Pno.
Vib.
Perc.
4 Tom-Toms (solo)
Bass
ff
fff

230
B♭ Cl. Solo
B♭ Cl. 1
E♭ A. Sax. 2
B♭ T. Sax.
E♭ Bar. Sax.
B♭ Tpt.
Tbn.
Pno.
Perc.
4 Tom-Toms
Bass
ff
fff

♩=♩ ma largamente!
B♭ Cl. Solo
gliss.
B♭ Cl. 1
E♭ A. Sax. 2
B♭ T. Sax. 1
2
E♭ Bar. Sax.
(open)
open
B♭ Tpt. 1
2
3
4
5
♩=♩ ma largamente!
Tbn. 1
2
3
4
solid
Pno.
Tom-Tom
Cym.
ad lib. (slow rock)
B. Dr.
slow drag
Perc.
(pizz.)
Bass

240
B♭ Cl. Solo
B♭ Cl. 1
E♭ A. Sax. 2
B♭ T. Sax.
E♭ Bar. Sax.
B♭ Tpt.
Tbn.
Pno.
Cym. ad lib.
Perc.
B. Dr. ad lib.
Bass

Bb Cl. Solo
Bb Cl. 1
Eb A. Sax. 2
Bb T. Sax.
Eb Bar. Sax.
Bb Tpt.
Tbn.
Pno.
Cym.ad lib.
Perc.
B. Dr. ad lib.
Bass
fff
p

(Poco a poco tempo primo)
250
Bb Cl. Solo
simile
Bb T. Sax.
Eb Bar. Sax.
sim.
Bb Tpt.
Tbn.
Bass
♩ = 160
solo
Eb A. Sax. 2
Pno.
Traps ad lib. as before
Perc.
p lightly

Bb Cl. Solo
Bb Cl. 1
Eb A. Sax. 2
Bb T. Sax. 1
Bb T. Sax. 2
Eb Bar. Sax.
Tbn. 3
Pno.
Perc.
Traps
Bass
p dolce
mf
Solo
mp dolce
mf marc.
260

Bb Cl. Solo
Bb Cl. 1
Eb A. Sax. 2
Bb T. Sax.
Eb Bar. Sax.
Tbn. 4
Traps
Perc.
Bass
270
pp
cresc.
mf
Solo
f
Bb Tpt. 1
Pno.
Vib.

B♭ Cl. Solo
B♭ Cl. 1
E♭ A. Sax. 2
B♭ T. Sax. 1
B♭ T. Sax. 2
E♭ Bar. Sax.
Solo
B♭ Tpt. 1
2
3
4
5
Tbn. 1
2
3
4
Pno.
Vib.
Traps
Perc.
Bass

Bb Cl. Solo
Bb Cl. 1
Eb A. Sax. 2
Bb T. Sax.
Eb Bar. Sax.
Bb Tpt.
Tbn.
Pno.
Perc.
Xyl.
Traps
Bass
tr
(f)
f

280
B♭ Cl. Solo
B♭ Cl. 1
E♭ A. Sax. 2
1
B♭ T. Sax.
2
E♭ Bar. Sax.
1
2
B♭ Tpt. 3
4
5
1
2
Tbn.
3
4
Pno.
Xyl.
Perc.
Traps
Bass
ff
più f

B♭ Cl. Solo
B♭ Cl. 1
E♭ A. Sax. 2
B♭ T. Sax.
E♭ Bar. Sax.
B♭ Tpt.
Tbn.
Pno.
Perc.
Traps
Bass

* This repeat should be made at least three times, and as many times as seems psychologically right (that is, to an "exhaustion point").

In tempo
1. 2. 3. or more
last time
Eb Cl. Solo
Bb Cl.
Eb A. Sax.
Bb T. Sax.
Eb Bar. Sax.
Bb Tpt.
Tbn.
Pno.
Timp.
Perc.
Xyl.
Traps
Cym.
Bass
non dim.
long
pp
ffff
fff

Nov. 4, 1949

LEONARD BERNSTEIN
DIVERTIMENTO FOR ORCHESTRA

Divertimento for Orchestra : *Instrumentation*

2 Flutes
2 Piccolos (Picc. 2 doubles Fl. 3)
2 Oboes
English Horn
Clarinet in E♭
2 Clarinets in B♭ (& in A)
Bass Clarinet in B♭
2 Bassoons
Contrabassoon

4 Horns in F
3 Trumpets in C
3 Trombones
Tuba (doubles Baritone Euphonium)

Percussion*
Piano
Harp
Strings

*Percussion instrumentation:
Timpani
4 Snare Drums (high to low)

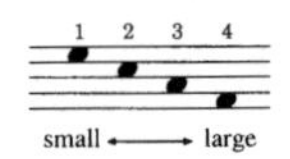

Bass Drum
Cymbals (pair)
Large Cymbals (pair)
Suspended Cymbal
Tam-tam
Triangle
Tambourine
Woodblock
2 Cuban Cowbells
(high & low)
Sandpaper Blocks
Rasp & Maracas
3 Bongos & 2 Conga Drums
4 Temple Blocks
Trap Set
Glockenspiel
Xylophone
Vibraphone
Chimes

Dedicated with affection to the Boston Symphony Orchestra in celebration of its First Centenary

Divertimento for Orchestra

I. Sennets and Tuckets

Leonard Bernstein
(1980)

© Copyright 1980 by The Estate of Leonard Bernstein.
Leonard Bernstein Music Publishing Company LLC, Publisher
Boosey & Hawkes, Inc., Sole Agent.

A
a2
Fls.
Picc.
Obs.
Eng. Hn.
Cl. in E♭
Cls. in B♭
Bass Cl. in B♭
Bsns.
Cbsn.
Hns. in F
1. Solo
Tpts. in C
Solo
Tbns.
Tuba
All snares off
4 Sn. Drs.
Tri.
arco
Vlns.
Vla.
Vcl.
Cbs.

B
Fls.
Picc.
Obs.
Eng. Hn.
Cl. in E♭
Cls. in B♭
Bass Cl. in B♭
Bsns.
Cbsn.
a2
ff
Hns. in F
a2
Tpts. in C
Tbns.
Tuba
(two players)
4 Sn. Drs.
Susp. Cym.
f
B
Vlns.
Vla.
Vcl.
arco
Cbs.

Fls.
Picc.
Obs.
Eng. Hn.
Cl. in E♭
Cls. in B♭
Bass Cl. in B♭
Bsns.
Cbsn.
Hns. in F
Tpts. in C
Tbns.
Tuba
4 Sn. Drs.
Susp. Cym.
Xylo.
Vlns.
Vla.
Vcl.
Cbs.
a2
ff
mf cresc.
f
cresc. molto
All snares on (4 players)
cresc.
molto
pizz.

C
Con eleganza
Fls.
Picc.
Obs.
Eng. Hn.
Cl. in E♭
Cls. in B♭
Bass Cl. in B♭
Bsns.
Cbsn.
Hns. in F
Tpts. in C
Tbns.
Tuba
Timp.
4 Sn. Drs.
Bass Dr.
Xylo.
Harp
Vlns.
Vla.
Vcl.
Cbs.
molto
sffz
a2
dim.
8va bassa
[snares off on drums 2, 3, 4]
(one player)
dim. molto
arco
p, preciso
pizz.

D
Fls.
Picc.
Obs.
(a2)
(2.)
Eng. Hn.
Cl. in E♭
Cls. in B♭
1. Solo
marc.
sub.
Bass Cl. in B♭
Bsns.
cresc.
Cbsn.
cresc.
Hns. in F
1. Solo
con sord.
2. Solo
con sord.
Tpts. in C
Tbns.
Tuba
4 Sn. Drs.
cresc.
Bass Dr.
cresc.
Harp
(D♮)
marc.
Vlns.
arco
Vla.
arco
cresc.
Vcl.
cresc.
Cbs.
div.
unis.
cresc.

E
Fls.
Picc.
Obs.
Eng. Hn.
Cl. in E♭
Cls. in B♭
Bass Cl. in B♭
Bsns.
Cbsn.
Hns. in F
Tpts. in C
Tbns.
Tuba
4 Sn. Drs.
Bass Dr.
Harp
Vlns.
Vla.
Vcl.
Cbs.
a2
f marc.
mp cresc.
cresc.
(I.)
senza sord. 1., 3.
(con sord.) 2.
senza sord.
(C♮)
div.
unis.
arco
brillante
(pizz.)
pizz.

Con gioia!
Fls.
Picc.
Obs.
Eng. Hn.
Cl. in E♭
Cls. in B♭
Bass Cl. in B♭
Bsns.
Cbsn.
Hns. in F
Tpts. in C
Tbns.
Tuba
Timp.
4 Sn. Drs.
Bass Dr.
Cyms. (pair)
Tamb.
Xylo.
Vlns.
Vla.
Vcl.
Cbs.
a2
cresc.
con sord.
(senza sord.)
ff con gioia
(1 player)
to Tri.
pizz.
arco

F
Fls.
Picc.
Obs.
Eng. Hn.
Cl. in E♭
Cls. in B♭
Bass Cl. in B♭
Bsns.
Cbsn.
Hns. in F
Tpts. in C
Tbns.
Tuba
Timp.
4 Sn. Drs.
Bass Dr.
Cyms. (pair)
Tri.
Xylo.
Vlns.
Vla.
Vcl.
Cbs.
a2
cresc.
senza sord.
con gioia
(damp)
loco
mp sub.
pizz.
arco
(non div.)

G
Fls.
Picc.
Obs.
Eng. Hn.
Cl. in E♭
Cls. in B♭
Bass Cl. in B♭
Bsns.
Cbsn.
Hns. in F
a2
ff
Tpts. in C
Tbns.
Tuba
[all snares off]
(2 players)
4 Sn. Drs.
Susp. Cym.
f
Vlns.
Vla.
Vcl.
Cbs.
arco

Fls.
Picc.
Obs.
a2
ff
Eng. Hn.
Cl. in E♭
ff
Cls. in B♭
Bass Cl. in B♭
Bsns.
Cbsn.
Hns. in F
Tpts. in C
Tbns.
Tuba
(all snares on)
4 Sn. Drs.
Xylo.
f
Vlns.
Vla.
Vcl.
Cbs.

Fls.
Picc.
Obs.
Eng. Hn.
Cl. in E♭
Cls. in B♭
Bass Cl. in B♭
Bsns.
Cbsn.
Hns. in F
Tpts. in C
Tbns.
Tuba
Timp.
4 Sn. Drs.
Bass Dr.
Susp. Cym.
Xylo.
Harp
Vlns.
Vla.
Vcl.
Cbs.
a2
mf cresc.
molto
cresc. molto
(4 players)
(Hard Timp. sticks)
(C maj.)
pizz.
arco
div.
non div.

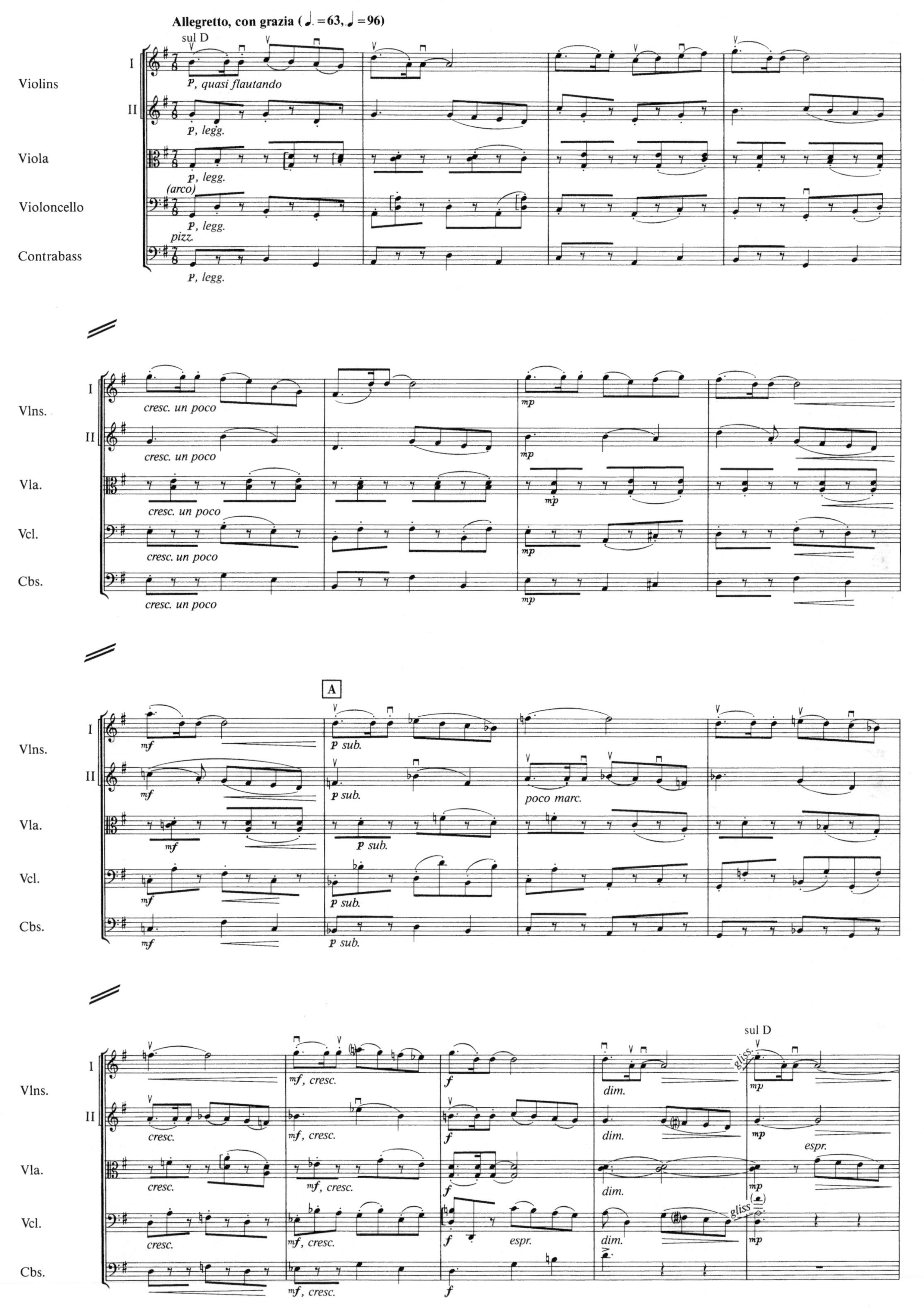
Allegretto, con grazia (♩. = 63, ♩ = 96)
Violins
Viola
Violoncello
Contrabass
sul D
p, quasi flautando
p, legg.
(arco)
pizz.
Vlns.
Vla.
Vcl.
Cbs.
cresc. un poco
mp
A
mf
p sub.
poco marc.
mf, cresc.
cresc.
f
espr.
dim.
mp
gliss.

Rit. (poco)

B **A Tempo**

Vln. I — Solo, gli altri
Vln. II — Solo, gli altri
Vla. — Sola, le altre
Vcl. — Solo, gli altri
Cbs.

p, delicato — pizz. non div. — *pp* — *cresc.* — *non cresc.*
pizz. *p, delicato* — non div. *pp* — *cresc.* — *non cresc.*
p — pizz. non div. — *mp, cant.*
mp, cantando — pizz. — *p, legato* — 1. Solo pizz. — *pp* — *non cresc.*

mf — *cresc.* — (sempre *pp*) — *cresc.*
mf, espr. — *cresc.* — (sempre *pp*)

C

f — *mf* — *pp sub.* — *cresc.* — (Tacet to **E**)
p sub. dolce cantando — *pp sub.* — *cresc.*
p sub. dolce — *PP sub.* — *cresc.*
mf

D
Vlns.
I
II
Vla.
Sola
le altre
Vcl.
Solo
gli altri
Cbs.
mf, cresc.
f
mf
dim.
arco div.
mf, dim.
poco gliss
mp, flautando
p
metà
con sord.
arco
1. Solo
(pizz.)
Rit. (poco)
pp
mp, flaut.
E
A tempo
Solo (senza sord.)
Vln. I
gli altri (con sord.)
Vln. II
Vla. (tutte) (con sord)
Vcl. (tutti) (con sord)
p, flaut.
pp, vibrando
div.
f sub.
pizz.
1.Sola
(senza sord.)
In tempo (non rit.)
flautando
dim. molto
sfz
f, dim.
arco unis.
mp, dim.
ppp

III. Mazurka

* All chords non arpeggiando, except the one 3 bars after [C].

Obs.
Eng. Hn.
Bsns.
Cbsn.
Harp
(f)
(Eb)
(Eb)
(Ab)
marc.
ff
cresc.
C
(in tempo)
ff
p sub.
f sub.
1.
p sub.
pp
(Eb maj.)
(Db)
(Db)
(Ab)
gliss.
sffz
molto Rit.
Molto più lento (♩= 72)
Solo
p, cant.
fp
pp
p
sf
l.v.

IV. Samba

Allegro giusto (𝅗𝅥 =96)
Flutes
Piccolo
Oboes
English Horn
Clarinet in E♭
Clarinets in B♭
Bass Clarinet in B♭
Bassoons
Contrabassoon
Horns in F
con sord.
Trumpets in C
3. Solo (open)
Brassy mutes
Trombones
1. Solo (open)
Brassy mutes
Tuba
con sord.
Timpani
3 Bongos
2 Congas
Bongos
Congas
(low)
(med.)
(high)
Rasp
Maracas
2 Cuban Cowbells
(low)
Suspended Cymbal
Allegro giusto (𝅗𝅥 =96)
Violins
Viola
Violoncello
(arco)
non div.
pizz.
div.
Contrabass

Fls.
Picc.
Obs.
Eng. Hn.
Cl. in E♭
Cls. in B♭
Bass Cl. in B♭
Bsns.
Cbsn.
Hns. in F
Tpts. in C
Tbns.
Tuba
Timp.
3 Bongos
2 Congas
Rasp
Maracas
2 Cowbells
(high)
Susp. Cym.
Vlns.
Vla.
Vcl.
Cbs.

A
Fls.
(loco)
a2
Picc.
(loco)
Obs.
a2
Eng. Hn.
Cl. in E♭
Cls. in B♭
a2
Bass Cl. in B♭
Bsns.
Cbsn.
Hns. in F
a2
Tpts. in C
Tbns.
con sord.
Tuba
con sord.
Timp.
3 Bongos
2 Congas
Rasp
Maracas
2 Cowbells
Susp. Cym.
Piano
A
Vlns.
f, brillante
Vla.
pizz.
div.
a3
Vcl.
pizz.
div. a3
Cbs.
unis.
arco
div.

Fls.
Picc.
Obs.
Eng. Hn.
Cl. in E♭
Cls. in B♭
Bass Cl. in B♭
Bsns.
Cbsn.
Hns. in F
Tpts. in C
Tbns.
Tuba
Timp.
3 Bongos
2 Congas
Rasp
Maracas
Susp. Cym.
Piano
Vlns.
Vla.
Vcl.
Cbs.
B
f cresc.
cresc.
ff
mp
mp, con eleganza
p
sempre con sord.
a2 con sord.
(brassy mute)
con sord.
pizz.
arco
unis.
div.
a3
sfz

Fls.
Picc.
Obs.
Eng. Hn.
Cl. in E♭
Cls. in B♭
Bass Cl. in B♭
Bsns.
Cbsn.
Hns. in F
Tpts. in C
Tbns.
Tuba
3 Bongos
Rasp
Maracas
2 Cowbells
Triangle
Piano
Vlns.
Vla.
Vcl.
Cbs.
ff sub.
a2
senza sord.
tight mutes
tight mute
(high)
(low)
(med.)
p legg.
arco
2. Soli
1. Solo
1. Sola
p molto
Tutti div.
Tutti
Tutte

C
Fls.
Picc.
Obs.
Eng. Hn.
pp
Cl. in E♭
Cls. in B♭
p sub.
Bass Cl. in B♭
Bsns.
p sub.
Cbsn.
Hns. in F
senza sord.
a2
f cant.
Tpts. in C
con sord.
a2 senza sord.
cant.
Tbns.
Tuba
Timp.
(hard sticks)
mf
3 Bongos
2 Congas
p, sub.
cresc.
Susp. Cym.
Sandpaper Blocks
2. Soli
1. Solo
Tutti unis.
Tutti
Tutte
Vlns.
1. Sola
Vla.
f, cant.
Vcl.
pizz.
arco
Cbs.

D Poco a poco accel.
Fls.
Picc.
Obs.
a2
Eng. Hn.
Cl. in E♭
Cls. in B♭
Bass Cl. in B♭
Bsns.
Cbsn.
mp, sub.
cresc.
Hns. in F
più f
Tpts. in C
Solo senza sord.
1. Solo senza sord.
Tbns.
Tuba
Timp.
3 Bongos
2 Congas
2 Cowbells
(low)
(high)
Susp. Cym.
Sandpaper
Blocks
Piano
D Poco a poco accel.
pizz.
arco
Vlns.
Vla.
Vcl.
Cbs.

Più mosso (𝅗𝅥 = 120)
a2
Più accel.
molto accel.
Fls.
Picc.
Obs.
Eng. Hn.
Cl. in E♭
Cls. in B♭
Bass Cl. in B♭
Bsns.
Cbsn.
Hns. in F
Tpts. in C
Tbns.
Tuba
senza sord.
Solo
Timp.
3 Bongos
2 Cowbells
(high)
Cyms. (pair)
Xylo.
Più mosso (𝅗𝅥 = 120)
arco
Più accel.
molto accel.
Vlns.
Vla.
Vcl.
Cbs.

Presto (𝅗𝅥 = 138)
flutt.
Fls.
Picc.
loco
Obs.
(a2)
Eng. Hn.
Cl. in E♭
Cls. in B♭
Bass Cl. in B♭
Bsns.
Cbsn.
p sub. cresc.
molto
più f
cresc.
Hns. in F
Tpts. in C
Tbns.
Tuba
Timp.
3 Bongos
Bass Dr.
Rasp
Maracas
2 Cowbells
Cym.
(high)
(pair)
(Susp. Cym.)
mf cresc. molto
Xylo.
sub. p
Vlns.
Vla.
Vcl.
Cbs.
pizz.
arco
div.
(pizz.)

Allegretto, ben misurato (𝅗𝅥 = 76)
Flutes
Piccolo
Oboes
English Horn
Clarinet in E♭
Clarinets in A
Bass Clarinet in B♭
Bassoons
Contrabassoon
Horns in F
Trumpets in C
con sord.
tight cups
Trombones
3. con sord.
Tuba
4 Temple Blocks
Wood Block
Piano
f, marc.
mf, dim.
p, dim.
Violins
Viola
Violoncello
Contrabass
pizz.

A
Fls.
Picc.
Obs.
Eng. Hn.
Cl. in E♭
1. Solo
(light accent)
Cls. in A
p, ma marc.
non cresc.
Bass Cl. in B♭
pp grazioso
Bsns.
p, ma marc.
Cbsn.
p, ma marc.
Hns. in F
Tpts. in C
Tbns.
Tuba
Piano
p grazioso
A
Vlns.
Vla.
1. Solo
(arco)
sul G
Vcl.
p grazioso
1. Solo
Cbs.
p

B
Fls.
a2
f sub.
ff
Picc.
f, marc.
Obs.
Eng. Hn.
Cl. in E♭
mf, marc.
Cls. in A
Bass Cl. in B♭
Bsns.
Cbsn.
Hns. in F
Tpts. in C
senza sord.
1. Solo
f marc.
2.
Tbns.
Tuba
Temp. Blks.
Choke Cym.
Traps
Wood Blk.
Bass Dr.
Piano
Vlns.
Vla.
Vcl.
Tutti
pizz.
Cbs.

Fls.
Picc.
Obs.
1. Solo
(light accent)
pp
Eng. Hn.
Cl. in E♭
Cls. in A
f, dim.
p
Bass Cl. in B♭
Bsns.
Cbsn.
Hns. in F
1. Solo
mp ma marc.
mf
Tpts. in C
Tbns.
Tuba
Temp. Blks.
mf, dim.
Wood Blk.
Vlns.
arco
pp staccatissimo
Vla.
grazioso
Vcl.
staccatissimo
Cbs.
1. Solo
(pizz.)

C
Fls.
Picc.
Obs.
Eng. Hn.
Cl. in E♭
Cls. in A
Bass Cl. in B♭
Bsns.
Cbsn.
(light accent)
1. Solo
ppp
non cresc.
mp
grazioso f
mp, marc.
p
(1. Solo)
f
Hns. in F
Tpts. in C
Tbns.
Tuba
Vlns.
Vla.
Vcl.
Cbs.
pizz.
Tutti

Fls.
Picc.
Obs.
Eng. Hn.
Cl. in E♭
Cls. in A
Bass Cl. in B♭
Bsns.
Cbsn.
Hns. in F
Tpts. in C
Tbns.
Tuba
Traps
Vlns.
Vla.
Vcl.
Cbs.
a2
mp cresc.
cresc.
mp sub.
molto
dim.
1. Solo con sord.
con sord.
(choke Cym.)
(Bass Dr.)
pizz.
p sub.

D
Non stringere
1. Solo
Fls.
Picc.
Obs.
Eng. Hn.
Cl. in E♭
Cls. in A
Bass Cl. in B♭
Bsns.
Cbsn.
bouché cuivré, ma trionfante
1,3 con sord.
2,4 con sord.
non cresc.
Hns. in F
(1.)
Tpts. in C
Tbns.
(con sord)
Tuba
non cresc.
soft stick
Timp.
(snare on)
Snare Dr.
Tenor Dr.
pp legg.
Traps
D
Non stringere
arco col legno
(pont.)
(legno)
(pont.)
(legno)
(pont.)
nat.
legno
nat.
legno
nat.
Vlns.
Vla.
Vcl.
Cbs.

E
Fls.
Picc.
1. Solo (cue, if needed, for Hn. Solo)
Obs.
pp
Eng. Hn.
Cl. in E♭
Cls. in A
mp
Bass Cl. in B♭
p
a2
Bsns.
ff
Cbsn.
Hns. in F
a2
senza sord.
Tpts. in C
senza sord.
Tbns.
senza sord. a2
Tuba
Timp.
Traps
Triangle
sffz
(steel hammer)
Chime
Piano
sul D
sul G
2. Soli
(nat.)
2. Soli
pizz.
flautando
Vlns.
Vla.
2. Soli
pizz.
Vcl.
arco
Cbs.

F
Fls.
Picc.
Obs.
Eng. Hn.
Cl. in E♭
Cls. in A
Bass Cl. in B♭
Bsns.
Cbsn.
senza sord. a2
Hns. in F
Tpts. in C
Tbns.
Tuba
senza sord.
hard sticks
Timp.
Temp. Blks.
Wood Blk.
Bass Dr.
(Large)
Large Cymbals
(pair)
Xylo.
Solo
Piano
mp, very square
senza pedal
Vlns.
Vla.
Vcl.
Cbs.

Fls. 1 2
Picc.
Obs. 1 2
Eng. Hn.
Cl. in E♭
Cls. in A 1 2
Bass Cl. in B♭
Bsns. 1 2
Cbsn.
Hns. in F 1 3 2 4
Tpts. in C 1 2 3
Tbns. 1 2 3
Tuba
Temp. Blks.
dim.
Wood Blk.
p
p
dim.
Xylo.
dim.
Piano
(non cresc.)
dim.
Vlns. I II
Vla.
Vcl.
Cbs.

G Pesante
Fls. 1 2
Picc.
Obs. 1 2
Eng. Hn.
Cl. in E♭
Cls. in A 1 2
Bass Cl. in B♭
Bsns. 1 2
Cbsn.
Hns. in F 1 2 3 4
Tpts. in C 1 2 3
Tbns. 1 2 3
Tuba
Timp.
Temp. Blks.
Wood Blk.
Bass Dr.
Cyms (pair)
Xylo.
Piano
Vlns. I II
Vla.
Vcl.
Cbs.
ff sub.
gliss.
a2
Tutti arco
sffz
pp
p

Fls. 1 2 a2 *ff*

Picc. *ff*

Obs. 1 2 *ff*

Eng. Hn. *ff*

Cl. in E♭ *ff*

Cls. in A 1 2 1. Solo *pp* *ff*

Bass Cl. in B♭ *ff*

Bsns. 1 2 a2 *ff*

Cbsn. *ff*

Hns. in F 1 2 a2 *ff* 3 4 a2 *ff*

Tpts. in C 1 2 a2 *ff* 3 *ff*

Tbns. 1 *ff* 2 3 *ff*

Tuba *ff*

Timp. *ff*

Temp. Blks. *p* *pp*

Wood Blk. *p* *pp*

Bass Dr. damp. *sffz*

Cym. *ff*

Xylo. *p* *pp*

Piano *pp* *ff*

Vlns. I pizz. *p* *pp* arco *ff*

II pizz. *p* *pp* arco *ff*

Vla. pizz. *p* *pp* arco *ff*

Vcl. div. pizz. *p* *pp* arco unis. sul G *ff*

Cbs. arco *ff*

* All winds play phrase in one breath, except flutes, where indicated.

Attacca

VII. Blues

Slow blues tempo (♩. = 56)
1. Solo
Trumpets in C (Jazz mutes)
f wailing
Trombones (Jazz mutes)
Tuba
(Ad lib. with brass, but spontaneous invention encouraged.)
l.v.
Trap Set
Sizzle Cymbal
Suspended Cymbal
Snare Drum
Tom Tom
High Hat
Bass Drum
f (rub with wire brushes)
Vibraphone
Piano
dolce vibrato
Tpts. in C
cresc.
p sub.
(all three to Harmon mutes)
Tbns.
p, tranquillo
(2. to Harmon mute)
p sub. dolce
dim.
[to Baritone Euphonium]
Tuba
lightly
Sizzle Cym.
Susp. Cym.
Sn. Dr.
Tom Tom
High Hat
Bass Dr.
(motor on)
Vibr.
mf, dolce
Piano
mf, dolce
Ped.

pochiss. rit. A tempo
A (♩ = ♩. prec.)
Tpts. in C
1. Take "Solo" mute
Solo
Tbns.
Solo *
Baritone
mp, singing
to Tuba
Trap Set
Sizzle Cym.
Susp. Cym.
Sn. Dr.
Tom Tom
High Hat
Bass Dr.
Vibr.
Piano
(Ped.)
* Longer phrasing preferred, if possible
B (♩. = ♩=prec.)
a2 *
Tuba
Solo break
(wood sticks)
(motor off)
f, marc.
* OSSIA: Trumpet I an octave higher (if guts and chops permit) until high G♯ 4 bars later.

* Piano plays directly after Susp. Cym.

Andante (♩ = 58)
Flutes
Large Tam-tam
p sempre
(non cresc.)
pp

A
B
Flutes
p
cresc.
mp
mf
mp, espr.

Segue MARCH
Flutes
Piccolo
Glockenspiel
Suspended Cymbal
cresc.
f
sempre f
molto
quasi f
p molto
pp molto
pp cresc.
mf molto

Doppio movimento
Alla marcia (𝅗𝅥 = 120)
[Fl. 3 take Picc.]
Flutes
Piccolo
Oboes
English Horn
Clarinet in E♭
Clarinets in B♭
Bass Clarinet in B♭
Bassoons
Contrabassoon
Horns in F
(Soli)
Trumpets in C
Trombones
Tuba
Timpani
4 Snare Drums
snares on top drum only
(1 player)
Cymbals (pair)
Suspended Cymbal
Glockenspiel
Piano
Harp
Doppio movimento
Alla marcia (𝅗𝅥 = 120)
Violins
Viola
Violoncello
Contrabass

flutt.
Fls.
a2
ff
cresc.
sff
C
f, brillante
Piccs.
(sempre a2)
Obs.
Eng. Hn.
Cl. in E♭
Cls. in B♭
Bass Cl. in B♭
Bsns.
Cbsn.
Hns. in F
fff
Tpts. in C
f, cresc.
Tbns.
Tuba
mf, sub.
Timp.
4 Sn. Dr.
mf cresc.
Bass Dr.
Susp. Cym.
Glock.
Vlns.
Vla.
f, marc.
arco
Vcl.
pizz.
Cbs.

Fls.
Piccs.
Obs.
Eng. Hn.
Cl. in E♭
Cls. in B♭
a2
a2
Bass Cl. in B♭
cresc.
Bsns.
cresc.
Cbsn.
con sord. a2 ritmico
cuivré
Hns. in F
con sord. a2
cuivré, legato
Tpts. in C
Tbns.
Tuba
4 Sn. Dr.
Bass Dr.
Susp. Cym.
Glock.
Vlns.
I
II
pizz.
Vla.
pizz.
Vcl.
Cbs.

Fls.
Piccs.
Obs.
Eng. Hn.
Cl. in E♭
a2
Cls. in B♭
Bass Cl. in B♭
Bsns.
Cbsn.
dim.
con sord.
a2
Hns. in F
f, cuivré
mp
f, cuivré, legato
dim. molto
Tpts. in C
Tbns.
Tuba
4 Sn. Dr.
Bass Dr.
Susp. Cym.
Glock.
Vlns.
Vla.
Vcl.
Cbs.
arco
pizz.

D
Fls.
Piccs.
Obs.
Eng. Hn.
Cl. in E♭
Cls. in B♭
Bass Cl. in B♭
Bsns.
Cbsn.
bouncy
(sord.)
senza sord.
Hns. in F
a2
Tpts. in C
Tbns.
Tuba
Timp.
4 Sn. Dr.
f marc.
Bass Dr.
(pair)
Susp. Cym.
Glock.
C♭maj., D♮
Harp
D
Vlns.
arco
Vla.
Vcl.
Cbs.

E
Fls.
Piccs.
Obs.
Eng. Hn.
Cl. in E♭
Cls. in B♭
Bass Cl. in B♭
Bsns.
Cbsn.
Hns. in F
Tpts. in C
Tbns.
Tuba
4 Sn. Dr.
Bass Dr.
Susp. Cym.
Vlns.
Vla.
Vcl.
Cbs.
a2
ff
fff
f
arco
pizz.

F Trio I
Fls.
Piccs.
Obs.
Eng. Hn.
dim.
Cl. in E♭
Cl3. in B♭
p, cant.
Bass Cl. in B♭
dim.
Bsns.
dim.
Cbsn.
Hns. in F
ff
mf
Tpts. in C
Tbns.
Tuba
4 Sn. Dr.
dim.
pp
(pp)
Bass Dr.
dim.
pp
Susp. Cym.
dim.
pp
Harp
F Trio I
Vlns.
p, cant.
dim.
Vla.
dim.
pizz.
Vcl.
dim.
Cbs.

Fls.
Piccs.
Obs.
Eng. Hn.
Cl. in E♭
Cls. in B♭
Bass Cl. in B♭
Bsns.
Cbsn.
Hns. in F
Tpts. in C
Tbns.
Tuba
4 Sn. Dr.
Harp
près de la table
A♭ maj.
marc.
stacc.
cresc.
pp!
Vlns.
Vla.
Vcl.
Cbs.
div.
unis.

G
Fls.
Piccs.
Obs.
Eng. Hn.
Cl. in E♭
Cls. in B♭
molto
Bass Cl. in B♭
cresc.
Bsns.
cresc.
Cbsn.
Hns. in F
Tpts. in C
Tbns.
Tuba
4 Sn. Dr.
pp!
cresc.
sim.
Harp
mp, marc. stacc.
G
Vlns.
cresc.
cresc. molto
molto
Vla.
cresc.
cresc. molto
Vcl.
cresc. molto
Cbs.
cresc. molto

Fls.
Piccs.
Obs.
Eng. Hn.
Cl. in E♭
Cls. in B♭
Bass Cl. in B♭
Bsns.
Cbsn.
Hns. in F
Tpts. in C
Tbns.
Tuba
4 Sn. Dr.
Bass Dr.
Susp. Cym.
Vlns.
Vla.
Vcl.
Cbs.
p, con eleganza
Piccolos stand up
a2 Soli
p, cant.
pp sub., con eleganza
pizz.
div.
mp, cant.
arco

H
Fls.
Piccs.
Obs.
Eng. Hn.
Cl. in E♭
Cls. in B♭
Bass Cl. in B♭
Bsns.
Cbsn.
Hns. in F
Tpts. in C
Tbns.
Tuba
4 Sn. Dr.
Harp
Vlns.
Vla.
Vcl.
Cbs.
p sub.
cresc.
a2
con sord.
3. Solo
p, marc.
(come prima)
mp, marc.
div.
unis.
arco

Fls.
Piccs.
Obs.
Eng. Hn.
Cl. in E♭
Cls. in B♭
Bass Cl. in B♭
Bsns.
Cbsn.
Hns. in F
Tpts. in C
Tbns.
Tuba
4 Sn. Dr.
Harp
Vlns.
Vla.
Vlc.
Cbs.
cresc.
sim.
p, marc.
div.
unis.

J
Fls.
a2
ff
sit down
Soli
Piccs.
Obs.
cresc.
molto
Eng. Hn.
Cl. in E♭
Cls. in B♭
Bass Cl. in B♭
Bsns.
Cbsn.
Hns. in F
senza sord.
Tpts. in C
p, cresc. molto
Tbns.
Tuba
Timp.
4 Sn. Dr.
Bass Dr.
Susp. Cym.
Glock.
Harp
(E♮)
unis.
Vlns.
Vla.
Vcl.
arco
Cbs.

Fls.
Piccs.
Obs.
Eng. Hn.
Cl. in E♭
Cls. in B♭
Bass Cl. in B♭
Bsns.
Cbsn.
Hns. in F
Tpts. in C
Tbns.
Tuba
Timp.
4 Sn. Dr.
Bass Dr.
Cyms (pair)
Susp. Cym.
Glock.
Harp
Vlns.
Vla.
Vcl.
Cbs.
a2
Soli
cresc.
ff
fff
f
B♮, G♮
pizz.
arco
p

K Trio II
Fls. 1 2
pp
(pp)
Piccs. 1 2
Obs. 1 2
Eng. Hn.
Cl. in E♭
Solo
p, dumbly
sempre p
Cls. in B♭ 1 2
p, dumbly
(p)
Bass Cl. in B♭
p, stupidly
(p)
Bsns. 1 2
Cbsn.
p, imbecilically
(p)
Hns. in F 1 3 2 4
con sord.
p, cretinously
a2
f
p
Tpts. in C 1 2 3
con sord.
f
con sord.
f
Tbns. 1 2 3
con sord.
f
con sord.
f
Tuba
f
Triangle
p
Piano
pp, stacc.
(pp)
Harp
Cmaj.
pp, stacc.
(pp)
K Trio II
Vlns. I II
pp
arco
f
pp
arco
f
Vla.
pp
arco
f
Vcl.
pp
arco
f sub.
Cbs.
pizz.
p
(pizz.)
f

Fls.
Piccs.
Obs.
Eng. Hn.
Cl. in E♭
Cls. in B♭
Bass Cl. in B♭
Bsns.
Cbsn.
Hns. in F
Tpts. in C
Tbns.
Tuba
Piano
Harp
Vlns.
Vla.
Vcl.
Cbs.
(pp)
p sub.
f sub.

L Tutti quanti tutta forza
Fls.
Piccs.
Obs.
Eng. Hn.
Cl. in E♭
Cls. in B♭
Bass Cl. in B♭
Bsns.
Cbsn.
Hns. in F
Tpts. in C
Tbns.
Tuba
Timp.
4 Sn. Dr.
Bass Dr.
Susp. Cym.
Glock.
Xylo.
Piano
Harp
Vlns.
Vla.
Vcl.
Cbs.
senza sord.
senza sord. [Bells up]
con bravura
pizz.
arco
sempre non div.
p sub.
8va

Fls.
Piccs.
Obs.
Eng. Hn.
Cl. in E♭
Cls. in B♭
Bass Cl. in B♭
Bsns.
Cbsn.
marcatissimo
Hns. in F
Tpts. in C
Tbns.
Tuba
Timp.
fff
ff
4 Sn. Dr.
Bass Dr.
Susp. Cym.
Glock.
Xylo.
(8va)
Piano
Harp
Vlns.
trem.
sempre non div.
Vla.
Vcl.
sim.
Cbs.

Fls.
Piccs.
Obs.
Eng. Hn.
Cl. in E♭
sempre tutta forza
Cls. in B♭
Bass Cl. in B♭
Bsns.
marcatissimo
Cbsn.
marcatissimo
Hns. in F
marcatissimo
Tpts. in C
Tbns.
marcatissimo
marcatissimo
Tuba
marcatissimo
Timp.
fff
ff
4 Sn. Dr.
fff
Bass Dr.
Susp. Cym.
Glock.
Xylo.
(8va)
Piano
(8va)
Harp
Vlns.
trem.
Vla.
marcatissimo
Vcl.
marcatissimo
Cbs.
marcatissimo

Vuota
Fls.
Piccs.
Obs.
a2
Eng. Hn.
Cl. in E♭
Cls. in B♭
Bass Cl. in B♭
Bsns.
fff marcatissimo sempre
Cbsn.
fff marcatissimo sempre
Hns. in F
sempre
Tpts. in C
gliss
sim.
Tbns.
marcatissimo sempre
Tuba
marcatissimo sempre
Timp.
4 Sn. Dr.
Bass Dr.
Susp. Cym.
Glock.
Xylo.
(8va)
Piano
Harp
Vuota
Vlns.
Vla.
Vcl.
Cbs.
marcatissimo
sempre

M
Fls.
Piccs.
Obs.
Eng. Hn.
Cl. in E♭
Cls. in B♭
Bass Cl. in B♭
Bsns.
Cbsn.
Hns. in F
Tpts. in C
Tbns.
Tuba
Tri.
Piano
Harp
Vlns.
Vla.
Vcl.
Cbs.
con sord.
a2 con sord.
pp,stacc.
(p) sempre
pizz.
arco
f sub.
(pizz.)

Fls.
Piccs.
Obs.
Eng. Hn.
Cl. in E♭
Cls. in B♭
Bass Cl. in B♭
Bsns.
Cbsn.
Hns. in F
Tpts. in C
Tbns.
Tuba
Piano
Harp
Vlns.
Vla.
Vcl.
Cbs.
pizz.
p sub.
f sub.

N Tutti quanti tutta forza
Fls.
Obs.
Eng. Hn.
Cl. in E♭
Cls. in B♭
Bass Cl. in B♭
Bsns.
Cbsn.
Piccolos stand up
All Brass stand up
senza sord.
Hns. in F
Tpts. in C
Tbns.
[Bells up]
con bravura
Tuba
Timp.
4 Sn. Dr.
Bass Dr.
Susp. Cym.
Glock.
Xylo.
Piano
Harp
Vlns.
Vla.
Vcl.
Cbs.
arco
sempre
non div.
sim.

Fls.
Piccs.
Obs.
Eng. Hn.
Cl. in E♭
Cls. in B♭
Bass Cl. in B♭
Bsns.
marcatissimo
Cbsn.
Hns. in F
marcatissimo
Tpts. in C
Tbns.
marcatissimo
Tuba
marcatissimo
Timp.
fff
ff
4 Sn. Dr.
fff
ff
Bass Dr.
Susp. Cym.
Glock.
Xylo.
Piano
Harp
Vlns.
trem.
sempre
non div.
Vla.
Vcl.
marcatissimo
Cbs.
marcatissimo

Fls.
Piccs.
Obs.
Eng. Hn.
Cl. in E♭
sempre tutta forza
Cls. in B♭
Bass Cl. in B♭
Bsns.
marcatissimo
fff marcatissimo
Cbsn.
Hns. in F
marcatissimo
fff
Tpts. in C
Tbns.
marcatissimo
Tuba
Timp.
fff
ff
4 Sn. Dr.
sffz
Bass Dr.
Susp. Cym.
Glock.
Xylo.
Piano
Harp
Vlns.
trem.
Vla.
Vcl.
Cbs.
marcatissimo

Sept. 10, 1980
(new ending: Sept. 1983)

SELECTED CONTEMPORARY SCORES

A complete list of our extensive library of contemporary scores is available on request. For more information about Boosey & Hawkes composers visit our website.

Michel van der AA
Here Trilogy

John ADAMS
Chamber Symphony
Short Ride in a Fast Machine
The Wound-Dresser

Louis ANDRIESSEN
Hadewijch
De Staat
De Stijl
De Tijd

Harrison BIRTWISTLE
The Cry of Anubis
Exody
Pulse Shadows
Theseus Game

Elliott CARTER
In Sleep, in Thunder
String Quartets nos 4 & 5
Triple Duo
Violin Concerto

Unsuk CHIN
Akrostichon-Wortspiel

Henryk Mikołaj GÓRECKI
Already it is Dusk
Kleines Requiem für eine Polka
Old Polish Music
Quasi una Fantasia

HK GRUBER
Aerial
Frankenstein!!

Magnus LINDBERG
Cantigas
Feria
Fresco

James MACMILLAN
The Confession of Isobel Gowdie
Veni, Veni, Emmanuel
The World's Ransoming

Peter MAXWELL DAVIES
Eight Songs for a Mad King
Orkney Wedding, with Sunrise
Symphonies nos 1–8

Steve REICH
The Desert Music
Different Trains
Tehillim

Christopher ROUSE
Symphonies nos 1 & 2
Trombone Concerto

Michael TORKE
Adjustable Wrench
Bright Blue Music
Ecstatic Orange

Mark-Anthony TURNAGE
No Let Up
Riffs and Refrains
Scherzoid

SELECTED SCORES

A complete list of our extensive library of classic 20th-century scores is available on request. For more information about Boosey & Hawkes composers visit our website.

Béla BARTÓK
Concerto for Orchestra
Piano Concerto No.3
Violin Concertos Nos.1 & 2
Divertimento
Sonata for 2 Pianos and Percussion

Leonard BERNSTEIN
Candide
Chichester Psalms
West Side Story

Benjamin BRITTEN
Les Illuminations
Peter Grimes
Serenade for Tenor, Horn and Strings
War Requiem
Young Person's Guide to the Orchestra

Aaron COPLAND
Appalachian Spring Suite
Billy the Kid Suite
Quiet City
El Salon Mexico

Frederick DELIUS
Appalachia
Sea Drift

Edward ELGAR
Pomp and Circumstance Marches
Sea Pictures
Cockaigne Overture

Alberto GINASTERA
Dances from Estancia
Variaciones Concertantes

Bohuslav MARTINŮ
Double Concerto
Symphonies Nos. 1-6

Serge PROKOFIEFF
The Love of Three Oranges
Piano Concertos Nos.2, 3 & 5
Violin Concertos Nos.1 & 2
Peter and the Wolf

Serge RACHMANINOFF
The Bells
Piano Concertos Nos.1-4
Rhapsody on a Theme of Paganini
Symphonic Dances
Symphonies Nos.2 & 3

Richard STRAUSS
Elektra
Salome
Four Last Songs
Der Rosenkavalier

Igor STRAVINSKY
Oedipus Rex
Petrouchka
The Rake's Progress
The Rite of Spring
Symphony of Psalms

Ad. 378

www.boosey.com